Landed! Proven Job Search .... Today's Professional

"We all lose our jobs, or our jobs lose us, and it is time to move on. Change is never easy but with *Landed!* in your hands, your odds just got WAY better. Randy Hain has seen it all, and he can share with you all you need to know to find the next great career in your life. Read it, believe it, do it! You will have no regrets."

> —**Chester Elton,** author of the New York Times best sellers, "The Carrot Principle" and "All In"

"Landed! is a must-read for both senior executives and recent graduates alike who want to take their career to the next level whether they are currently in a job or looking for the next one. Randy provides keen insights from his own experience while summarizing helpful 'best practices' from his vast network of experienced corporate leaders, HR professionals and entrepreneurs. Take great notes because *Landed!* is full of tips that really work!"

> —**Tim Tassopoulos,** executive vice president of operations for Chick-fil-A

"As a college student looking at a tough job market in a few years, I appreciate the practical lessons here. I want to find the right job and best fit for me and think this book can help. I appreciated the sections on interviewing and negotiating. Definite must read for students and anybody looking for a new job."

> —**Brian Anthony,** student at Clemson University

"As a graduate of job transition, I am thrilled to see this book released. The skills that need to be developed and matured in order to identify and earn a new job are critical skills that will benefit any professional throughout their career. Randy's latest book walks the reader through detailed discernment that should be completed regularly, even for those of us not looking to make a move. To successfully manage your career, it take measurable goals, a plan and the right tools. This book is a necessary tool and one that will inspire as much as coach."

> —**Paige S. Barry,** senior vice president at Fiserv and founder of Little Flower Job Search Assistance

"Randy Hain has once again taken a thoughtful and practical approach to the job search process. He truly captures the fundamentals that every job seeker should encompass in today's competitive marketplace. This is a must-read before you embark on your job search journey!"

> —**Ed Wolff,** chief operating officer at Cortland Partners

"*Landed!* is a 'must read' for those in transition ... good for the job search, good for the soul! Randy Hain brings new life to a scary time, sharing his personal advice from years as a professional networker/recruiter and augmented with recommendations from expert interviews. *Landed!* is a great mix of professional guidance, personal assessment and positive encouragement. Readers will find it refreshing and practical with a great blend of do's and don'ts and heart felt motivation."

> —**Terry Trout,** vice president of service delivery for Cbeyond and member of board of directors for Women in Technology

"Whether you are a college student or experienced professional, in order to successfully navigate today's complex, rapidly evolving workplace, you need to develop a proactive plan to communicate your value add, manage your network and engage in meaningful work. Randy has leveraged his unique professional insights, personal career journey and passion for helping others to help readers develop a timely, yet practical approach to launching an effective job search that will help you move from 'in-transition' to *Landed!*"

> —**Jason Aldrich,** Ed.D., executive director of the Career Management Center at Georgia State University's Robinson College of Business

"*Landed!* presents a holistic view of job and career search with a proper focus on first understanding who you are before charging headlong into the routines and practices that are frequently more clichés' and distractions than help. Accurate road maps are hard to find but this one matches the traveler with experience and guidance from those who know."

> —**Allan J. DeNiro,** senior vice president and chief people officer, Haverty Furniture Companies, Inc.

"Randy's suggestions for helping find your next and best career move resonate for leaders at any level and stage in their career. His expertise with LinkedIn as a tool proves helpful to any professional whether contemplating a move or already in career transition."

—**Karen Bennett,** senior human resources executive with YP

"In *Landed!*, Randy Hain has delivered a comprehensive blue print for a successful job search grounded in the realities of today's business and social media landscape. Not only does he provide up to date advice and tools for your search, but he also focuses on the personal and psychological impact of the search process and gives practical solutions for coping. *Landed!* is a great resource that I highly recommend to those people working through the job search process."

—**Patrick Devlin,** vice president of human resources - global technology at Alere, Inc.

"Another outstanding book! Randy Hain, in his accessible, pragmatic style, has written a well-organized guide to professional fulfillment. He grounds his counsel in a philosophical framework then offers nuts and bolts tools for the job search process, offering prescriptions on topics such as relationship building, networking, resume writing, interviewing and negotiating. He draws from his own well of wisdom then taps into the expertise of a broad range of insightful industry experts. The result is a thought provoking road map for achieving job search success."

—**Pam Beckerman,** senior director of human resources with Jabian

"A modern day job search is not what it used to be and luckily Randy Hain and his new book is here to help. There is both an art and science to finding one's next career move and *Landed!* covers it from the inclusion of the science (immediately applicable tools, scripts and techniques to move forward) to what has become even more important to a meaningful career move ... the art. The art requires more than most job seekers realize. Randy invites in experts to weigh in on everything from the psychological factors that are critically important for success to how to "give and take" appropriately with one's network. The world is growing increasingly more complicated so mastering the art of the job search as Randy recommends will be the differentiator going forward."

—**Dr. Karen Steadman,** founder and CEO of Leadership Futures, Inc.

"I love this book! Anytime I can find a combination of inspiration and practical handles within the same read, I recognize it as a rare find. Throughout the pages of this short book, you will be touched and inspired by the authentic heart that so marks the life and pen of Randy Hain while at the same time, you will get doable practicalities for making a transition from yesterday's job to tomorrow's opportunity."

> **—Terry R. Barber,** CEO and chief inspiration officer of Performance Inspired, Inc. and founder and chairman of Jamstir, Inc.

"Randy Hain's newest book, *Landed!*, is just what the doctor ordered for job seekers. It goes beyond finding the right match for your skills and gets you to think about what is really important to you when assessing positions. With a blend of proven ideas, interviews and questions, *Landed!* provides a thoughtful perspective of what will really make that next job one were you can thrive and be a success."

> **—Beth Armknecht Miller,** Vistage Chair and talent management advisor for Executive Velocity

"Randy Hain's new book, *Landed!* is the most comprehensive and insightful work on the subject I have read. It is absolutely packed with simple and practical wisdom that will equip and inspire job seekers to move forward in a purposeful way. Best of all, much of the advice offered is useful not only for the job seeker, but for anyone looking to fully maximize their work and life experience."

> **—Larry Mohl,** founder/CEO of Jamstir Inc., co-author of *Wall Street Journal* best seller, "Networking is Dead: Making Connections that Matter"

"In his latest book *Landed!*, Randy Hain offers a rare combination of information for anyone seeking a first, last, new or different job. He deftly weaves the practical requirements (resumes and interviewing) with the psychological (self-assessment and signature strengths) with the personal (networking and LinkedIn) with the theoretical (pros and cons of self-employment). Randy leverages his vast work experience into a single framework, and I can think of no other resource with such scope and value."

> **—Paul J. Voss,** Ph.D., professor at Georgia State University and president of Ethikos

"As practical as it gets ... *Landed!* is like having your own job search coach. Randy Hain translates nearly two decades of executive search expertise into step-by-step advice for a successful job search. This book will change the trajectory of your search and give you the knowledge and confidence to land that dream job."

> **—Price Harding,** partner at CarterBaldwin Executive Search

"This method works! If you are starting a job search or looking to proactively manage your career, *Landed!* is the best career management book out I have read in a long time."

> **—Mimi Vold,** vice president of human resources for Facet Technologies LLC

"Randy has done a great job with this topic. His extensive experience in search and in modern networking comes together well in this practical, actionable book. While clearly a great resource for those in transition or considering a job move, this should be read by anyone who wants to actively manage their career."

> **—Brad Cummings,** sr. vice president of human resources for Tandus/Centiva and Tarkett Sports

"As a former 27-year corporate executive with a Fortune 50 company, I am the epitome of Randy Hain's new book, *Landed!* It is more important than ever to be deliberate in managing your career path - no one else will. Randy offers practical and logical steps to achieving your next position, whether with another company or charting a path of your own - as I did. I wish I had this book a year ago!"

> **—Timm Rader,** Activus Sales Consulting

"Randy has written the must-own book for anyone in career transition or contemplating a new job. Today's job market moves quickly, is extremely competitive, and relies on technology. It's intimidating just to get started! *Landed!* is the guide (and Prozac) for anyone who is scared about where to start or how to land a job in today's market. Randy's years of experience in recruiting and coaching combined with the written testimonials of professionals who hire or have successfully gone through career transition themselves make this book incredibly valuable to read and continually reference."

> **—Matt Tovrog,** partner of Bell Oaks Executive Search

"Having spent the past 15 years in the executive search business I can honestly say *Landed!* captures many of the themes I have used over the years when I have advised professionals at all levels from recent college graduates to seasoned professionals in transition. The book does a superior job of pulling everything together in terms of the many pieces of the puzzle to consider when attempting to execute a successful job search. I plan on recommending this book to the professionals I work with regarding their job search. I am excited to have such a strong tool to use along with my counsel!"

> **—Todd Warshaw,** partner of Bell Oaks Executive Search

"It's rare to find an author and a book that gives the reader such proven and practical advice as well as Randy has done with *Landed!* Not just for the job seeker, *Landed!* should be read and followed by anyone interested in managing their career. Randy's thoughtful combination of his experience and the experiences of other successful professionals gives us a wonderful handbook for taking control of our job searches – whether they be internal promotions or new adventures. This is a must read!"

> **—Amelia Fox,** co-founder of Spotlight Performance

Landed!

Proven Job Search Strategies for Today's Professional

Randy Hain

FOREWORD BY BRANDON SMITH

SERVIAM PRESS

ISBN: 1489557946
ISBN-13: 978-1489557940

SP

SERVIAM PRESS

Published by
Serviam Press, LLC
www.serviampress.com

DEDICATION

I dedicate this book with love and appreciation to Saint Joseph, the Patron Saint of Workers.

CONTENTS

ACKNOWLEDGMENTS

This book has been on my mind since early 2011 and I am excited to finally offer job seekers a useful tool which I firmly believe will help them in a meaningful way. I have been humbled and gratified by the positive response to *Landed!* from colleagues and peers who knew about the project. The encouragement and helpful advice of friends and family has long been behind the successful completion of all my books, but this one in particular.

The book would not have been possible without the expert editing and project management of Lisa Tilt, president of Full Tilt Consulting. Lisa's insights and enthusiasm for the project kept me going forward when I could have easily put this on the back burner because of my busy schedule. Lisa is a great friend and outstanding professional - I hope we do another book together in the future.

I am very grateful for the people who contributed their experiences and insights as candidates, hiring managers and marketplace experts. My sincere appreciation to Angela Naphin, Andrew McGowan, Natalie Cheney, Andrew Dietz, Jo Ann Herold, Dean Harbry, Andrea Chilcote, Keith Hicks, Don Sather, Dr. Kym Harris, Vicki Hamilton, Dr. Patty Kubus, Greg Jackson, Allen McNeill, Susan O'Dwyer, Virginia Means, Sam Robb, Randy Patterson, Michael Thomas, Nancy Vepraskas, Dr. Ron Young, Jodi Weintraub, Russ Wise, Michael Esposito, John Reetz, Lori Dubuc, Mike Jones and Paige Barry.

Thank you Dr. Tim Elmore, Nicole Siokis and Dr. Jason Aldrich for your expert and helpful contributions to the Appendix section of the book.

The book cover was designed by Karen Daniel of Red Tusk Studio. I have collaborated with Karen and her husband, Ed, for years and love tapping into their creative genius!

My friend, Brandon Smith (The Workplace Therapist), contributed the excellent Foreword for the book and quotes in various chapters. His expertise on tackling workplace dysfunction and consulting experiences inside dozens of companies was an excellent contribution to the book.

I would like to say thank you to my Bell Oaks Executive Search business partners, Price Harding, Todd Warshaw and Matt Tovrog for their encouragement and friendship. Also, my sincere thanks to Carol Chizzolin of Bell Oaks for her ongoing support all these years.

Finally, I wish to warmly thank my wonderful wife and sons for their love, support and giving me a reason to go to work and do my best every day. Sandra, Alex and Ryan – I love you very much.

FOREWORD

I got the text early on a Saturday morning. It simply read, "Call me. I need to talk." My heart sank. I instantly knew what it meant. Michael had been laid off. After nearly 30 loyal years with the same employer, he was in job search mode for the first time in his career. Michael was in shock, but if he was gut-level honest with himself, he saw this coming. In fact, for over a year, Michael had seen the writing on the wall – a demotion into a role he had held 15 years prior, mass layoffs across his company, and a new boss from "the outside" that appeared to not like him from day one.

Like most of us, Michael didn't want to face the daunting possibility of resetting his career. So, in the face of fear and uncertainty, Michael did nothing. He didn't network. He didn't draft a resume. He didn't search job boards. He waited and remained loyal to his employer, hoping that this story might have a happy ending. Unfortunately, Michael's time ran out and the choice was made for him on an unassuming Friday afternoon.

Monday, the first official day of his job search, came all too quickly. Michael woke up, poured himself a cup of coffee, sat down to his outdated personal laptop and stared at the screen. Networking, resumes, LinkedIn, recruiters, positioning - it was a swirling tidal wave of "to do's" that was crashing down on him. Where to start? What to do? How long will it take? And, if figuring out the next step wasn't enough, Michael still needed to address the emotional impact of being let go.

"Fired," Michael quietly whispered to himself. Never had his confidence received such a debilitating blow. He always thought of himself as a valuable player at his company. He thought they loved him and the feeling definitely was mutual. Michael bled the company colors as evidenced by the dozen golf shirts, coffee mugs and other knick-knacks he had that were emblazoned with the company logo. But now he had to face the cold hard truth that the feeling wasn't mutual.

Like any soured relationship, he no longer felt wanted or valued. His identity and confidence were shaken. "I can't interview like this," he thought. And then there were Kate and the kids. Kate, his wife of nearly 20 years, was not taking Michael's transition well. She had questions for Michael that he simply couldn't answer. What were they going to do? What was his plan? Would they have to move? "No, we aren't going to move," she would quickly announce in a desperate attempt to gain some control over what was happening. She didn't want to uproot herself or the family from their support system.

Pressure, stress, anxiety, depression - Michael was feeling it all. He needed help but didn't know where to turn and who to ask. He felt like going back to bed in hopes that he would wake up and find himself in a different story with a different ending.

Michael's tale is not an unusual one. Whether we find ourselves in Michael's circumstances or we are trying to prevent a similar fate, having a clear plan in place is the antidote and prescription to turning unexpected disappointment into profound opportunity. And yet, there are very few resources that truly help address the issue of both planning for and landing the next job, until now. What Randy Hain has so wonderfully brought to the working world is a perfect prescription for how to take control of one's career and life.

From asking each of us the deep questions of finding meaningful work to the tactics of how to build valuable relationships, construct professional networks and master LinkedIn, Randy gives each of us the gift of empowerment in *Landed!* Through Randy's decades of experience working with leaders in transition at all stages of their careers, he knows what works and what doesn't. He's seen it all. In a very real and practical way, Randy gives each of us the gifts necessary to blueprint our careers and take action so we can have the careers and lives that each of us has always wanted.

Follow Randy's prescription and I guarantee there will be no layoff, downsizing or unexpected office closure that will slow your career journey. His guidance will help you craft a plan, strengthen your network and boost your confidence in a way that will naturally catapult you to something greater.

The choice is clear Make the next stage of your career and life what you've always wanted it to be. Now is the time. Not yesterday. Not tomorrow. Today. With *Landed!* at hand, I'm certain you can have the career and life of your dreams. *Take the first step today.*

Brandon Smith
"The Workplace Therapist"
www.theworkplacetherapist.com

INTRODUCTION

There is no shame in losing your job - it will likely happen to many of us at some point in our careers. Look at it as an exciting opportunity to take stock of your life and a rare chance to be more intentional about the next move in your career. Over the last two decades, through my current role as a partner with Bell Oaks, a respected national executive search firm, and previously as head of recruiting for a billion-dollar restaurant company, I have had the opportunity to interview thousands of candidates around the country. Many of the men and women I meet are specifically recruited for searches my firm is running for our clients, but the vast majority are referred from my large network and others seeking us out because of our reputation for treating candidates professionally and offering candid and helpful advice.

As you can imagine in these challenging economic times, there is a sizable population of good people affected by corporate layoffs and downsizing. There is also a growing group of passive job seekers who are seeking better career opportunities on their own initiative as well. Over the years, I have observed several characteristics about these individuals:

- Other than "getting back to work" or finding a better job, they are often unsure of what they really want from their careers or how to achieve their goals.
- Their personal networks have often been neglected while they pursued their careers, and they are often starting job searches without a sizable or accessible source of friends and business colleagues to ask for help.
- They don't have resumes or what they currently have is not presentable.
- They are inexperienced at interviewing.
- They have not kept current with hiring trends or growth industries.
- Effective use of social media in their job search is daunting to them.
- Networking may be awkward and difficult.
- Asking for job search assistance is often uncomfortable.

- They believe search firms help candidates find jobs, when in fact, most search firms are hired by companies to fill open positions.
- There is a strong sense of urgency to find a new job quickly due to financial reasons.

Although outplacement assistance is available to some candidates, it is not a benefit all enjoy. Sometimes the outplacement assistance received by downsized employees is of questionable value and results in little more than an upgraded resume. Many candidates seek out professional coaches or pay companies to market their resumes in order to find them jobs. There are certainly a few quality career coaches around, but they can be cost prohibitive for many candidates. Do your homework before engaging a career coach and make sure what they're offering is truly what you need.

Be leery of firms who promise to market your resume for money - I have never heard of anyone getting a new job this way. These companies charge sizable fees and I am very skeptical of the value provided for such a high cost. Being out of work likely means you have finite financial resources, so spend your money wisely.

So, where does that leave a candidate in need of a job?

Quite simply, you need an effective game plan and a proven approach to job search. In this book, I share some of the insight and experience I have gathered over the years on how to effectively begin and conduct a job search. There is no guarantee that a new job will be a direct result from these suggestions, but I can offer the unique perspective of someone who has interviewed thousands of candidates and counseled hundreds of clients.

Through my experiences and candid interviews with job seekers, hiring managers and helpful experts, I am hopeful you will find the right strategy and practical tools in this book to help you secure your next position. Just as important, I hope the search for your new job helps you clearly identify your top priorities and allows you to pursue a life filled with purpose and meaning.

I wrote this book for <u>you</u>, whoever you are, and I sincerely hope it is a source of comfort and help along your career journey.

Good luck!

Author's Note: You might find it very helpful to keep a job search journal as you read this book. Each chapter has questions for reflection and an action item to complete, and reading your responses collectively once you've completed the book may offer some valuable information on what you truly seek as a professional.

SECTION I

SELF-ASSESSMENT

1 WHAT AM I REALLY LOOKING FOR?

You went to college to learn accounting or study engineering. Maybe you majored in communications or political science. Possibly, you were a college athlete with aspirations to join a professional league after school. Maybe you have earned an MBA. We often approach our college years with a career in mind only to find ourselves way off track from our original goal just a few years later. Why?

In my personal experience and through observation, I believe many of us only get a glimpse of the work we enjoy or desire to have after a few years of experimentation in the workforce. To the lucky few who knew at 18 what they wanted to do for the rest of their lives (and actually did it), I salute you. For the rest of us who needed to experience years of trial and error, I share your pain. When I was 18, I had aspirations of using my political science degree and four quarters of Russian from the University of Georgia to work in the Foreign Service or CIA. When I was 22, climbing the corporate ladder, making a good living and having a family were much more important to me.

What's your story? What are you looking for now, at this point in your life? If you are looking for a new job, what do you hope to find in your next role?

Finding a job and a company that provides everything on our wish lists is a tall order. Sometimes we expect too much and when we don't get it, frustration set in. Let's not be naïve and assume our job will bring total happiness. I assure you it will not and I wrote about this very subject in my book, Something More: The Professional's Pursuit of a Meaningful Life.

Among the candidates I meet, ranging from recent college graduates to senior executives in transition to employed potential job seekers, a central theme is present in most conversations: the desire to "have it all" in their career. They want that next role to have a checkmark next to each box on our "ideal" job list. There may be exceptions, but generally speaking, very few jobs are able to meet these expectations. So where does that leave us? Consider these eight areas before making a change or accepting a new position:

1. Do a skills inventory. What are your competencies and specific areas of expertise? What do you have to offer that is unique or sought after? Are you applying these skills to your current job, or do you feel underutilized? Will the new job you are considering maximize your skills?

2. Do a needs inventory. What specific requirements do you have that are not being met in your career? Is it intellectual stimulation? Mentoring? A position that challenges you? Higher income? A loftier title? More balance? Flexible hours? Whatever is on your list should be realistic (a new convertible BMW company car is unlikely!) and something you have the courage to discuss with your current manager or future employer.

3. Identify repairs needed. What are your development areas? Be honest about what you need to work on professionally and personally. Consider if you are getting this assistance in your current role, and how you might get it in a new position. Please be forthcoming here, otherwise you cannot hope to get the help you are seeking.

4. Are you aligned? Does your chosen career field utilize your education and training? Does your compensation history align with your experience and market value? Are you on an appropriate and realistic career trajectory?

5. What are the expectations? A common mistake made by

those dissatisfied at work is "the failure to clarify what is expected of them," says Brandon Smith, business consultant, executive coach and founder of *The Workplace Therapist* (www.theworkplacetherapist.com). "Most would rather guess than discuss it with a manager, and when that happens they usually guess wrong and end up frustrated," says Smith. Additionally, it's important to know what in turn is expected of your boss since this is helpful in making your own expectations clear.

6. What are you passionate about? This is important – I believe most of us want to feel that what we are doing is worthwhile and making a positive difference. Make a list of what ignites your passion and determine if your current job or future role will allow you to pursue your noble, overarching goals.

7. Do your homework. Perform your due diligence on the marketplace. What companies align with your values? Where will your skills be valued? What companies have an inspiring vision? Go beyond Google and company websites – reach out to friends in your network and utilize social media sites (LinkedIn is the best option) to connect with people inside these organizations to get a more realistic picture. You owe it to yourself to not neglect this critical step.

8. Are your values in sync with your job? This is an area we should never have to compromise, but too often people mask their true nature and personal values for the sake of their career. Ask yourself if you are free to be your authentic self at your current workplace, or if you feel compelled to make unhealthy compromises in order to fit in. If looking for a values match in a future job, ask questions to understand what is deemed important to the hiring manager and the organization.

Working in tandem with the eight-point checklist are two significant mindset shifts which will not only make this reflection process easier, but also make you more effective professionally (and personally).

1. **Practice self-awareness.** It is a gift granted to very few, but the good news is – it can be acquired. Comparing your current behavior to your internal standards and values, and

acknowledging your strengths, weaknesses and desires can help you in every aspect of your life. There are countless personality tests available: DiSC, Birkman, Hogan, Myers-Briggs, etc. Become an objective evaluator of your current and past job performance, how your peers and company leaders perceive your work, and how you interact with others. If you're not sure, ask them. Remember that if you find yourself considering a career change every few years, the one obvious and constant thread through each change is you.

2. **You touch it, you own it.** More than a decade ago, I was vice president of recruiting for a national restaurant chain. We had a saying within the culture, "You touch it, you own it!" In a nutshell, you were empowered to act like an owner. Even if you had little direct responsibility for a particular issue or problem, you were expected to act like you owned all of it. No excuses, no complaining and no blaming others – just do what you had to do to achieve the goal or fix the problem. It taught me the valuable lesson of taking personal responsibility for my actions and doing everything in my power to make things better. I also learned the importance of influence versus control and how I could create positive change, even when I did not have direct authority.

Seeking more insight into the subject of what we are really looking for, I reached out to a well-respected executive advisor and coach, Dean Harbry. Dean is the founder and president of Internal Innovations (www.internalinnovations.com) and has counseled numerous leaders over the years on their business performance and career goals. Here are the highlights from an interview with him.

Dean, based on your extensive experience as an executive coach and consultant, what do you frequently observe about candidates in career transition? Are there common threads?

"They seem to fail to take the long term approach to career management. It's not unusual for them, once they've Landed their next job, to be tempted to allow their personal network to grow cold and to stop thinking about what comes after that new position. My counsel to them is that it's unlikely that this job is the destination – it's more likely that it's just the next step in a long journey. Managing one's career with extended time horizons in mind is the key to successful career management."

You mentioned that many people are not sure what they are looking for. What is your advice for someone like this?

"Dig deep, be clear about your own values and personal mission, and determine compatibility in any of the options that surface. I have them complete a process to determine critical success factors and non-negotiables in any possible new job assignment. Then they rate each opportunity against that list. No job is going to be perfect – it's a series of tradeoffs. Which ones are most important, and which ones are okay to let go of? This creates awareness regarding fit, but provides some wiggle room for the best possible job given the options."

In your estimation, do a majority of people looking for new roles take stock of their lives and reflect before jumping back into a new job?

"Most people lack guidance and don't know the right questions to ask. This is where someone can benefit from a coach. I ask the tough questions and get them thinking about and declaring what is most important and how certain jobs fit into their purpose and calling. Work/life balance is the measuring stick that helps to center career decisions for many professionals. These questions are usually not considered by those in transition suffering from anxiety when seeking the next job assignment. Provision and family responsibilities tempt the unemployed to settle for something less. Family and friends need to assist those in transition by reinforcing work/life principles, bringing the long term into view."

What about the perspective of a real job seeker? As I was pulling together my thoughts for this book, I encountered a marketing communications executive named Angela Naphin, a former Fortune 50 company leader who was in her first job search in 15 years. I was interested in gaining a fresh perspective from a new job candidate on how she determined what she was looking for in a new position.

Angela, as a successful marketing and communications professional with a long tenure, what have been the biggest challenges for you during your job search?

"It doesn't happen overnight! I had been with the same company for so long that it's taken time to establish my personal brand and to understand the Atlanta job market again. My title did not translate to other companies well and it was difficult to decipher what position level I was seeking. I was very clear about the roles and responsibilities in interviews, but I had several false starts with companies because of unclear job descriptions and salary expectations.

"I am willing to take the necessary time to find the right role for me, and I'm using the time off as a period of personal rejuvenation and growth. This transition is a gift. I am learning new skills, meeting amazing people and am having the time of my life.

"Part of my brand is giving back. It is hard for me to see people suffering through their transitions. I want to help. Therefore, I have taken what I have learned and created job search training modules. I am teaching classes on networking, social media and resume writing. Even if you have a job, you need to nourish your network and prepare for the next opportunity. It is my way of paying it forward."

Considering that you haven't had to look for a new job in several years, has this job search been a steep learning curve for you?

"Yes. As a successful executive, mother and community volunteer, I have not spent much time expanding my business network. I had to shift my focus and think about my contacts in a very different way. I have a wide network, but interacted with people mostly in my role as a volunteer, church Elder or involved parent. Now, I am calling them for a different reason, but the relationship is there and everyone has been very willing to offer feedback, coach me and send referrals.

"It feels like a lifetime ago since I interviewed last and the approach is completely different now. The social media revolution has altered the way people find jobs. You have to be current and have a presence online in a big way. With that said, it is your networking connections that will land you a role, not the Internet. A combination of both is the right strategy."

As you ponder my observations earlier in this chapter, Dean's thoughts and Angela's recent experience, be mindful that going through the process of identifying and understanding what you really want out of a job and a career is quite involved. It requires hard work and commitment. A common mistake I see with many job seekers is, after losing a job, they focus exclusively on finding the identical job with a different company. Financial pressures may necessitate finding a new job quickly, but you can always take enough time to do your homework, learn of new opportunities available today (especially if you've been out of the job market for years) and ask exploratory questions of both yourself and the new company.

Questions for Reflection:

1. Before reading this chapter, did I really consider what I desire out of my life and career? If I am honest with myself, do I really know what I want? Why or why not?
2. Randy Hain advocates making lists and taking inventory of who I am and what I must improve on in an effort to be more self-aware. Am I aware of my strengths and shortcomings? Do I find it painful or easy to be open about these things?
3. Dean Harbry advocates viewing your career as a long journey with stops along the way. Is this how I have done it to date? Why or why not?
4. Angela Naphin has developed a clear and practical approach to her job search and seems clear about what she wants. Does her approach resonate with me? If not, how might I do it differently?

Action Item:

As you reflect on the lessons of this chapter, begin thinking through how you will identify what you are looking for and write up a first draft of your approach.

2 WHAT OBSTACLES ARE IN MY WAY?

I am an observer. People fascinate me and I enjoy listening to their stories, challenges and triumphs. I have interviewed and spoken with thousands of individuals in career transition over the last two decades, and these interactions have helped me develop a clear opinion about the obstacles that often deter people from landing a new job. Let's call these obstacles "land mines."

The image in your mind right now is probably of someone stepping on a hidden explosive device buried in the ground in a jungle war zone. In a job search, there are an endless series of land mines, often of our own making, which prevent well-intended candidates from reaching their goal of a new career opportunity.

In my opinion, these fall into three distinct categories: *Fear*, *Stuff Your Friends Should Tell You* and *Predictable & Avoidable*.

Fear

Fear can be paralyzing. Accompanied by desperation and financial pressures, it can be almost unbearable. I see candidates in transition all the time who are dealing with some form of fear, and they are either unaware of the problem or don't know how to address it. Here are some examples:

- *Fear of conflict.* Conflict avoidance is rampant at every company and certainly among job seekers. We want to avoid offending or bothering others who can help with a job search, and as a result opportunities for positive engagement are lost. Fear of conflict also prevents one or both parties from speaking with candor and transparency.

- *Fear of rejection.* A very common and universal fear to be sure. It is closely associated with fear of conflict. Candidates shy away from asking friends, former coworkers and others in their network for assistance because a negative response may result in embarrassment. They also fall short of diligently and aggressively pursuing job leads with potential employers for the same reason. Each rejection compounds the problem for the job seeker and grows in intensity over time.

- *Fear of the new or unknown.* Many job seekers find themselves woefully unprepared for a job search when they begin. Technology, new methods of networking, social media options and new interviewing techniques – the list of changes seems endless and can be overwhelming. Many people don't even know where to start.

Helpful Tip: Start by identifying what you are afraid of. Being self-aware enough to list your strengths and weaknesses is critical. We must recognize and understand our fears if we hope to conquer them. Of the "land mine" categories I have listed, this is the most challenging one. But, ask yourself these questions: What will happen if I don't overcome these fears? Is my fear of being unemployed stronger than my fear of conflict, rejection and the unknown?

John Reetz, president of JR Media Solutions Group and a former job seeker himself, offers this insight: "Don't let paralysis set in. Any job change is a challenge, and the best way to confront it is to immediately get back out there, offering your skills and expertise."

Stuff Your Friends Should Tell You

There are likely people in your life who are helping and advising you to some degree on your job search. Call them friends, call them accountability partners –the important thing is to have people with whom you can share ideas, frustrations and have candid conversations.

A recurring issue I've seen for years with candidates is a surprising lack of candid advice and insight they receive from their network of friends and fellow job seekers. It is likely related to the fear of conflict we already identified and is absolutely detrimental to the process.

Here are a few examples of feedback your friends and peer should share with you. Keep these in mind as you engage in conversation with them and use these as ways to encourage their candor:

- "Your resume needs work." I see countless resumes that need significant work to make them more appealing and up-to-date to prospective hiring managers. Often, the changes are simple: have a clear and unambiguous objective, list quantifiable accomplishments, don't embellish, limit resume to two pages, etc. Share your resume with others and ask them for honest feedback. They may not want to hurt your feelings, but they are actually hurting your job search more by withholding the truth.

- "You are coming across as desperate and needy." Nobody wants to share or necessarily hear this feedback, but many would benefit from this coaching. Every week without a paycheck and every month of lowered self-esteem only fuels desperation. It is completely understandable, but channeling that desperation to a networking contact or in an interview will result in disaster.

- "Stop letting pride and ego get in the way." Compromise is an ugly word for many people. In a job search, you may have to compromise on title, income, scope of the role and possibly geography in order to find a new position. Project and consulting work should also be up for consideration. Candidates sometimes need to hear this, especially at the beginning of a job search when they see no reason why they should have to accept a lesser title or income. Don't let your ego get in the way of a good opportunity – you never know where those can lead.

- "Stop waiting by the phone." This is a popular path for candidates: send their resume out to a few companies, post it on Monster.com, build a profile on LinkedIn and then ... wait. In this economy, jobs will not come looking for you.

Brandon Smith, The Workplace Therapist, offers this advice: "I often meet individuals in transition who hold a reactive orientation toward both their search and how they approach their resume. It is as if they are saying, 'Here I am, now you tell me what I should do for you.' This approach will almost always conjure up fear and anxiety because we are waiting for others to determine our fate. What if they don't pick me? What if they don't see what I can do? How long will it be?

"Rather, I would encourage those in transition to ask, 'Why does the world need me today more than ever?' Use the answer to that question to fuel you, give you a sense of purpose and mission, and make your resume and job search more purposeful and proactive. The difference will be clear."

Helpful Tip: Carefully select accountability partners, not just close friends who will speak the truth. You need that candor and a heavy dose of reality while in career transition, not sugarcoated platitudes (see Chapter 14).

Also, always analyze what you are doing and determine if you are being effective. Be willing to switch gears and try new things and above all, don't blame the economy for everything. You play the most important role in your job search and a little self-awareness coupled with straight talk from candid friends and partners will help a great deal.

Predictable & Avoidable

I am constantly amazed by how job seekers are caught unaware when they lose a job. There is a surprising lack of preparedness and the reasons vary: ignoring negative industry trends and news, discounting poor company performance leading to layoffs, or suffering from "it couldn't happen to me" syndrome. This inattentiveness continues to manifest in a job search that is unsuccessful.

Here are a few of the predictable and avoidable mistakes I have seen over the years:

- *Starting a job search without a viable network.* As I address in more detail in Chapter Five, leaving a job and having to build a network from scratch is a significant issue for so many job seekers. We get comfortable at work and ignore the necessity of staying connected to old classmates, former work colleagues, industry counterparts, etc. These networks are the best resource for landing a new position, yet many candidates spend the first 60 to 90 days of a job search simply building a brand new list of contacts. This is completely avoidable if we maintain strong networks whether we are employed or not.

- *Putting all your eggs in one basket.* You hear about a great job opportunity that is a good fit and put all of your energy and time into pursuing this role. Weeks go by, you go through the interview process, are named a finalist and then they offer the job to another candidate. Yikes! You just wasted weeks of time focusing on this one opportunity instead of aggressively pursuing multiple leads. Don't stop until you have a written offer in your hand. Common problem, easy to avoid.

- *Time, attitude and effort.* It's likely a job search will take longer than you anticipate. Magic rarely happens and you need to be emotionally, financially and mentally prepared. As we discuss in the next chapter, attitude is everything. Despair will creep in if you are not careful – stay positive. A job search is actually a full time job and requires maximum effort for you to be successful.

- *Being unable to "brand" yourself.* Knowing how to appropriately sell yourself and your skills is critical in a job search and yet, most people I encounter struggle with this challenge. You are at your best when you are doing what? What is your value proposition? What have you become known for?

Figure out how to sell yourself and your brand early in your transition.

Mike Jones, a former Fortune 50 marketing executive who was in transition a few years ago, shared this insight from his job search: "It took me some time to realize that I was initially struggling with my search and transition. I was a senior executive from an industry-leading company who worked on branding and positioning multi-million dollar brands. And yet, I couldn't accurately describe myself in a concise manner for others to understand."

Helpful Tip: In an age of predictable economic cycles, when company loyalty to employees cannot always be counted on and downsizing is commonplace, we need to accept that nobody is immune to being laid off. We need to do the best we can in our careers, but be well prepared for the possibility of unexpected career transition.

The key is to maintain strong networks, stay abreast of current trends and technology, continually work on building your personal brand and be prepared for the seemingly fateful pink slip I hope you never receive. Looking for a new job can be a long, distressing journey that may tax your financial, physical and emotional resources. Preparation, active listening and learning from mistakes will help you minimize these obstacles.

My intent in sharing this chapter is to help people in career transition overcome the self-created obstacles that make landing a new role more difficult. This list doesn't encompass the totality of land mines you may encounter, but these are the ones I find to be recurring themes.

Consider this helpful insight from Nancy Vepraskas, president of respected human resources consulting firm, *P2Excellence*, who has witnessed job transition from both a company and personal perspective: "A job search, like all major life changes is a marathon event. It's important to stay physically and mentally fit, and pace yourself for the long miles ahead."

The changing economy is a formidable problem for the job seeker today as the news isn't always that great and it is easy to feel deflated about your efforts. However, professionals are getting new jobs every day in spite of that. Think objectively about your actions, mindset and results, and determine if you are potentially creating the land mines I described. The goal is to find a great new role as quickly as possible, and it is my sincere hope that by identifying these obstacles and removing them early in a job search, you will accomplish this in a shorter period of time. Remember, the best way to avoid stepping on a land mine is to avoid planting one in the first place.

Another professional who has observed these obstacles that often derail the job search process is Andrea Chilcote, president of Morningstar Ventures, a Phoenix-based firm specializing in leadership and executive development and change consulting. Andrea's work as an executive coach affords her the opportunity for insight into the personal drivers of career success. Here is some of her insight:

Andrea, as a well-respected business consultant and executive coach, I am curious to get your opinion on the self-limiting factors which may get in someone's way as they look for new roles. Which are the most common?

"The most significant self-limiting factor may be failure to follow one's heart. You might be thinking that's a Pollyannaish notion, so let me clarify. I'm not suggesting that, for example, the artist-at-heart quit her corporate finance job to pursue a dream of watercolor painting, leaving a mortgage and her children's education at risk. I do know that when we're faced with opportunities to do something new, we're often bombarded by internal messages cautioning us to take the route that's safe, predictable and possibly most lucrative. It's important to sort those messages from what we really want (and need) to feel purposeful and productive in life.

"More than ever, I'm meeting and working with courageous individuals who are taking the time to examine what's best for them personally, as well as how they can strongly contribute in whatever new role they assume. Often that's a dilemma in itself, yet one better faced with eyes (and heart) wide-open.

"I can give you two examples. One is a senior leader who

considered slowing his career progression to literally have more rest and recreation. He soon realized that what he does as a leader literally ignites life in people and thus his business. That, at least for now, is the spark for his own life.

"Another is a relatively young executive who has worked in the same industry her entire career. From her perspective, the ability to make a difference in her own company was limited while the ability to affect true change was a core driver and a key talent. But there was a voice inside her that questioned whether she really had the qualifications to lead elsewhere. Once she boldly identified her talents, experience and passion (and quieted the self-limiting voice), she Landed the perfect role."

How important is self-awareness in being effective in a job search? Why?

"In my opinion it's impossible to do what I'm describing – examine what's uniquely right for you – in the absence of understanding the kinds of things that engage and motivate you, as well as the things that create stress. In the case of a job search, self-awareness is just the first step. We have to become self-aware in reference to others (such as a new boss), and in reference to the corporate culture.

"I know an intelligent and gifted middle manager who is about to move to a new firm after only three months in what she might have described as a dream job. The problem? Her boss, one of the company owners, is a self-declared lone wolf who doesn't collaborate (and openly admits it). This manager would tell you that three months ago she thought she could change this about the company because to her, the benefits of teamwork are self-evident. She now admits that was a naive perspective and is 'interviewing' her new prospective employer through this lens."

How can job seekers avoid "getting in their own way" as they look for their next career? Can you offer a short list of ideas to help in avoiding self-inflicted mistakes?

"Be cautious of whose counsel you heed. Here's a test. Is the other person suggesting what they would do if *they* were you, or giving you objective advice based on what's right for *you*? Family members are particularly guilty of this well-intended yet damaging perspective. I'm certainly not suggesting you pay no attention to the needs and feelings of those affected by your choices, but more suggesting that you sort those and consider each alongside your own instincts. Consider whether your well-meaning friends are speaking to you or really to themselves or their self-interests.

"A coach can be one of the most valuable resources during times of transition. This can be a paid professional or a truly objective colleague who can act as a thinking partner, sounding board and trusted advisor. Sometimes others can help us see our true nature and the choices available if we're bold enough to act on them."

So, we begin to clearly see the negative impact obstacles can have on the job search. What about the perspective of an active job seeker? I reached out to Natalie Cheney who I interviewed in the summer of 2013 for her insights on these obstacles and what she had learned during her search process. Natalie was most recently a Vice President of Professional Services/ Customer Services for startup Software as a Service (SaaS) Organizations. She recently Landed a similar role in another organization.

Natalie, as you reflect on your recent job search, what did you identify as obstacles in your search? What came between you and the next job?

"One of the key obstacles I identified early on was recognizing that I really networked well in my previous companies, but they were small startups and therefore the network was small. I found when I moved from startup to startup with individuals in my small network, it never really grew. When I was ready for my next job move, the employer organizations of my contacts did not excite me nor did the opportunities. The size of my network was quite an issue for me. Quite simply, I didn't network outside my organization because I was 'busy' focusing on my career inside the walls of the small organizations where I worked.

"Another challenge for me was related to timing. I began reaching out and targeting certain companies in my 'target company group.' This worked well and resulted in many positive phone conversations and meetings, but the positions just were not available at the time. But I continue to keep these leads warm.

"Finally, one of the biggest challenges in the job search was to convince hiring managers and recruiters that my abilities spanned broader than the titles I held previously. Since my experience was in Customer Service, Consulting and other similar positions, those were the roles they wanted to put me in. In hindsight, I should have changed my positions to get the 'variety' of titles under my belt."

How did you deal with the "emotional roller coaster" of a job search? What is your advice for other job seekers on dealing with these particular challenges?

"There were definitely good search days and bad search days. I recognized that looking for the right job is in itself a full-time job, and if you are not careful, everyday life can distract you. Treat it like a job, wake up at the normal time, keep personal distractions at bay, etc. Being a Type A personality and not utilizing your skills or having your brain challenged is difficult. The entire process has been humbling as I recall the success I have had and the hard work I put into my career.

"For sanity's sake, I found that having other personal goals and objectives helped me not feel like the walls were caving in. I focused on achieving the goals I already had in place but hadn't focused on given my full-time position: caring for two little girls and being a good wife. For the last eight to 10 years, eating right and exercising weren't priorities, so I wanted to change that as well. Making progress on these goals helped keep me balanced and relatively calm, especially when the job search was not going well. This is absolutely a mental game.

"One last thing, I like to measure progress, and that can be difficult in a job search. I treated it like a sales job where my progress was tracked by the volume of connections I made each week. Connections included meeting for coffee or lunch, holding phone conversations, connecting at events, etc."

What were the biggest surprises for you in your job search?

"I was surprised when I didn't get hired in the first 30 days of looking. I was always in high demand. I was shocked and wondered what was different. I could execute any plan with style, grace and passion. I was strategically involved in selling the two startups companies I worked for. Surely there were tons of companies that needed my skillset! The problem was, no one knew who I was, what I could bring and that I was available. The surprises that I experienced during this recent job search will not catch me unprepared again."

As we've learned in this chapter, there will likely be obstacles standing between you and your new job. The challenge is to minimize the ones of your own making. Based on what you've read, what are the obstacles you now see in your path? More importantly, how will you move them out of the way?

Questions for Reflection:

1. Andrea Chilcote stressed the need to be self-aware about our personal challenges and the obstacles of our own creation. Am I self-aware? Am I doing something with this knowledge?
2. The author identified fear as one of the aspects of a job search that can be paralyzing. What am I afraid of and why? Is this fear greater than the fear of remaining unemployed?
3. Does Natalie Cheney's recent job search adventure resonate with me? Were her surprises similar to ones I have experienced?
4. Do I have a personal brand? Can I clearly articulate my brand to others?

Action Item:

Reflect on the lessons in this chapter and make a list of the identifiable obstacles in your way. After reading the book, develop your plan for overcoming each obstacle.

3 THE PSYCHOLOGY OF A JOB SEARCH

Here is the good news: you will not be subjected to psychoanalysis in this chapter. The "psychology of a job search" refers to the mindset, strategy and general attitude you have as you engage in finding your next role. As I have observed over the years, negative viewpoints, defeatism and a lack of self-confidence can undermine your efforts as can overconfidence, arrogance and stubbornness.

I sought out two experts who I respect greatly to help me capture what is most important about job search psychology: Michael Esposito and Dr. Patty Kubus. First, Michael Esposito serves as Vice President of Human Resources, in-house employment counsel and "Hambassador" for The HoneyBaked Ham Company of Georgia, Inc. and as such leads all of the organization's HR functions. Here are some of his insights:

Michael, in addition to your role as a respected senior HR executive, you have selflessly given your time over the years to work with countless professionals in transition and speak to job networking groups. As you reflect on your experiences, what are your thoughts on the "psychology" of a job search?

"It is important for candidates to come to peace with why they are in transition so they can proceed on their job search journey unencumbered with negative baggage. For example, if they are angry, bitter or grieving over their job loss, it will be difficult to present themselves in a positive, upbeat fashion to prospective employers or to their network. They will also become a psychological burden to their friends and loved ones. In sum, candidates must be able to learn from the past so they can move forward optimistically and authentically."

How can professionals in transition avoid the extreme emotional highs and lows of a job search? Do you have any examples in mind where this challenge has derailed candidates from getting jobs?

"Individuals often experience highs and lows while in transition because they have not honestly faced the *past* (perhaps they are in transition because of poor performance), the *present* (unrealistic assessment of their opportunities in the job market, as in a shrinking demand for their skill set) and the *future* (such as the possible necessity of relocation). Oftentimes, this leads to emotional extremes. For example, sometimes candidates will experience unrealistic highs simply because they have an interview when, in fact, they are only one of many candidates in a marketplace where employers are looking for 'the perfect fit.' Conversely, some candidates will repeatedly get down when they are passed over despite being, in their mind, a 'perfect fit.'

"Candidates would do well to understand the realities of their own marketability in a challenging (and global) work environment and learn how things really work. That takes time, effort and self-awareness. In sum, the sooner candidates realize that searching for and securing a job is like riding a roller coaster, the sooner they can brace themselves for the ride – and hopefully even learn from and enjoy it."

What mindset do you coach job seekers to have as they look for a new role? Is there a game plan or strategy you recommend?

"The mindset I encourage candidates to adopt is that they alone are responsible for finding a job, no one else. The conversation usually starts with three questions: What do *you* want to do? Where do *you* want to do it? And what's *your* plan (or strategy)? Candidates should think long and hard about developing honest and realistic answers to these questions before beginning their search; and that includes applying for jobs, engaging in informational interviews, and networking. They may wish to enlist the help of a panel of trusted advisors to provide them with feedback or to engage a career coach who can continually challenge them, their actions and their strategy. At the end of the day, candidates need to invest in their journey from both a financial and emotional perspective. They need to build a plan and work the plan. When working the plan isn't delivering the desired results, the candidates need to develop and execute a new approach."

Anyone who knows Michael Esposito is familiar with the years he has spent speaking to job ministry groups and working tirelessly to help individuals find new jobs. He has offered a dose of tough love in this chapter, but his candor is spot on and brings clarity to an issue many job seekers face.

My next interview is with Patty Kubus, Ph.D., president of Leadership Potential International, Inc. (LPI). LPI is a leadership consulting company that specializes in executive assessment for both selection and development. It is her firm's philosophy that everyone desires to reach their potential by using their unique talents and skills to bring value to their organizations.

With her education, training and experience, Patty has a unique perspective as she has long been a consultant inside companies that understand the pressures her clients face each day and why they sometimes move on to pursue new positions.

Patty, there is a certain psychology behind the job search process that we have both witnessed over the years. Can you speak to this from your experience?

"The most important element to any job search is your mindset. Fortunately, you have complete control over your mindset. This is really good news since there are so many aspects of a job search over which you have little control, such as the number of job openings, the economic state, your competitors' skills and experience, a prospective manager's likes and dislikes and biases. It is pointless to spend time worrying about things that you cannot control.

"Why is a positive attitude so critical? Your attitude determines your behavior. If your attitude demonstrates that it is just a matter of time before your skills, experience, education and personality are matched with the perfect job, then your behaviors will mirror what is necessary to make that happen (assessing yourself, creating an outstanding resume, networking in-person and on LinkedIn, preparing for interviews, getting references, following-up). A positive attitude will give you the energy to do the necessary work.

"A positive attitude will also help you make a favorable impact on the people you meet. You can have stellar credentials, but if you are not projecting energy, enthusiasm and interest, you are likely to be passed over. Your body language communicates who you are far more than your words and resume. Your voice, gestures, eye contact and posture are a direct reflection of what is going on inside you. People can 'fake' positive body language for a short while, but a good interviewer will want to spend a reasonable amount of time with you, and unless you are a professional actor, you cannot fake positive energy for very long. It all starts on the inside, and it is under your control."

How can job seekers effectively manage their way through this emotional roller coaster?

"Maintaining a positive mindset is critical and is actually easier than you might imagine. But it does take some awareness and effort. Your goal is to develop:

- *A positive attitude* – which drives how you come across to others, as well as how much energy you have to do what you need to do.
- *Resilience* – some people are more durable than others, but there are things you can do to build your resilience (see below).
- *Humble confidence* –be aware of your talents and skills as well as your shortcomings. No one is great at everything.

"How do we build these traits in ourselves? Here are a few suggestions:

- *Gratitude.* Every day there are usually many things to be grateful for. Identify them daily. Make a conscious effort to be grateful for what you have.

- *Acceptance.* It is easy to accept our blessings, but more challenging to accept things that did not go our way. Reframe those disappointments and accept that 'it wasn't the best for me right now.' Know that something better is on its way. Believe it and feel it.

- *Mindfulness.* Be aware of how you view situations, your emotions and how you talk to yourself. Keep your self-talk positive. Remind yourself what is under your control and what is not.

- *Solution-focus.* Focus on what you can do, not on the problem or what is out of your control.

- *Reflection.* Think about how you have handled disappointments in the past. Ask yourself: How did I react? Is this typical for me? Is this an effective behavior? What helped me move on? What can I do to move on faster in the future? Learn from the past, but don't dwell on it.

- *Health.* This goes without saying that maintaining a healthy lifestyle (nutritious food, exercise, sleep, hobbies, etc.) will help you feel better physically, emotionally and mentally and will help build your resilience, confidence and help you maintain a positive attitude. Keep balance in your life.

- *Social Support.* While some of us are more extroverted (gaining energy from being around people) than others, we can all benefit from sharing our highs and lows with friends. It is amazing how a good friend can help boost your spirits and help you to reframe a situation that may appear devastating to you.

"In general, you need to manage yourself: your thoughts and emotions rather than being controlled by them."

There is a growing group of people who have given up and have convinced themselves they can't find meaningful work. It is difficult to get out of this emotional tailspin. What is your advice for someone who feels there is no hope in finding a job?

"My advice is this: you were born with unique skills, talents, strengths and interests. There is only one you, and you were put here to use those talents. There is a great job out there for you.

"If that job is not manifesting itself to you, ask yourself some important questions:

- *Am I clear on my skills, talents, strengths and interests?* If you are not sure, ask a professional to help you. There are many well-designed inventories to help you clarify what you are good at. Ask people who know you – friends, teachers, co-workers, managers and former managers, family. People love to share their insights and most likely would be happy to help you.

- *Are my expectations too high or too low?* Ask yourself if you are qualified for the positions you seek. Do you have the requisite skills, experience and education/certifications? On the flip side, if you are applying for jobs for which you are overqualified, you will encounter frustration. If managers see you as overqualified, they know you might become bored quickly, be unproductive or even leave.

- *Am I coming across in interviews in a positive light?* You might consider role-playing an interview with a colleague. There may be behaviors you exhibit during an interview, of which you are unaware, that may be negatively interpreted. Some of these common behaviors mentioned by hiring managers include: talking too much, not listening, displaying arrogance, using body language which shows a lack of interest (poor eye contact, monotone voice, slouching posture, over or under using gestures, not dressing professionally), and not being prepared with examples of accomplishments, questions and knowledge of the company and industry. Get some coaching and practice before your next interview."

Can you recall a specific example of someone who successfully navigated through these psychological challenges to land a new role? What stands out most about this person in your mind?

"I knew a man who decided to leave his job and move to a new city, for personal reasons, which was several hundred miles away where he knew virtually no one. He began a new position six months after relocation. From all the ideas listed above, here are the actions he took that helped the most. This job seeker:

- was very clear on his strengths, skills and talents
- was very clear on the type of job he wanted
- had a good, basic resume that clearly showed his skills
- networked everyday with people who touched his desired industry
- maintained a healthy life style
- built a network of social support in the new city and, this is the most important one, he <u>knew</u> that there was a great job out there for him and <u>knew</u> that it would just be a matter of time. He stayed optimistic and patient.

"Focus on the steps you need the most, and those that will help you the most. The person described above was very extroverted and really enjoyed networking. Not everyone does. You might need to focus on your emotions and building resilience, or on identifying your strengths. Maybe you need help on setting realistic expectations. Your attitude is paramount to a successful job search."

Even though this chapter addresses mindsets and attitudes in a job search, I encourage you to also consider the impact the search may be having on your spouse, children, friends and others in your network. They are likely feeling almost as anxious as you are. Be honest with your inner circle, but take a balanced approach as you share information and updates. For example, "I had a really tough interview today, but I have two more next week that look promising." They are your support team, and as unfair as this may seem, they are looking to you for signs of positive encouragement.

The job search may possibly take months, not weeks. The search process is a marathon and not a sprint, so prepare yourself emotionally, mentally and spiritually for what lies ahead.

Questions for Reflection:

1. After reading this chapter, how would I describe my mindset/attitude? How has it affected my efforts to find a new job?
2. Michael Esposito stresses that job seekers alone are responsible for their job search. Does this resonate with me? Have I been blaming others for my lack of progress?
3. Dr. Patty Kubus is encouraging as she shares her belief that there is a great job out there for each of us. Do I believe this? If not, what are my answers to her questions assessing the obstacles?
4. Dr. Kubus believes we all control our own mindsets. Do I believe this? What can I do to change mine?

Action Item:

In your job search journal, write about your current state of mind. Be honest about your attitude and mindset with regard to your job search and consider how you might be affecting others around you. Refer back to this after you complete the book and in the days ahead as a point of reference.

SECTION II

THE NETWORK

4 THE UNCONNECTED LEADER

Failing to build an effective network can have a long-term negative impact on a career. I have come across this phenomenon many times in my professional life, and most recently in conversations with professionals who have unexpectedly found themselves in career transition.

Networking is more than creating a safety net for an inevitable period of career transition. It is a means to access an enormous pool of resources with unlimited benefits. The reason business professionals stop networking is manifold, and I will address many of those in this chapter. More importantly, I will speak to the investment required, as well as the payoff for those who do it well. On a related topic, the next chapter addresses how to network with intention so that the opportunities we create are immediately capitalized on in an effort to find viable job opportunities.

The Barriers

Why is networking a challenge for many business people today? What or who gets in the way? Most often, we do. Here are five fundamental barriers that we create for ourselves when it comes to building a network:

1. **"I don't have enough time."** This is the easiest to overcome as you will see in the investment section of this chapter. It's simply a scheduling and commitment issue.

2. **"I just don't see the importance."** Andrew Dietz, president of Creative Growth Group, shares his view: "For many leaders, networking is an interior project, if it is done at all. On the exterior of the business, there are only 'vendors' or 'customers,' so why network with them? And, despite all the talk of innovation, there persists a 'not inventive here' culture in many corporations and professional services firms."

3. **"My job is secure, so I don't need to spend time meeting new people."** Unfortunately, I have seen many leaders who felt safe in their positions fall victim to corporate downsizing. This false sense of security was once rampant, but it just isn't the reality of today's workforce.

4. **"I'm on Facebook and LinkedIn, so I am networking."** These helpful social media tools serve a useful purpose and can enhance the process. But, they are just that – tools. A hammer isn't going to nail something to the wall without your participation. Similarly, building a network won't happen without some level of face-to-face interaction.

5. **"I'm not very good at making new connections and in fact, find it intimidating."** This is a troublesome, and common, admission for many. Remember that networking can and should be tailored to your style and personality. The secret is to find the method that maximizes your strengths.

Helpful Tip:

I find the best way to alter a point of view is to ask challenging questions. For example: Does my team have the best talent available, or where will I find great people in my next role? Am I getting the personal development I need? Is my job secure and if not, do I have a network of people who can help me? Do I have quick access to helpful professional resources and competitive intelligence?

If you answered "no" to any of these questions, this chapter was written for you.

The Investment

Okay, you understand the importance of networking and its potential barriers, so what comes next? Networking must be a priority, so rethink your calendar. Be selfless and help others.

Make personal interaction the ultimate goal versus simply connecting via the Internet. Vibrant networks take time to build and a long-term commitment to sustain and grow them.

Here are five practical ways to make a meaningful investment in you networking efforts:

1. **Take an honest look at your calendar.** There are five opportunities a week for coffee/breakfast, and five opportunities a week for lunch. Start utilizing at least one of these times to schedule a weekly meeting with someone new. You have to eat, so you accomplish two things with the effort of one.

2. **Make time for existing contacts in your network, both within and outside your organization.** Nurture these relationships while expanding new ones. Also, ask these people for connections to new contacts in order to build a larger, more relevant network.

3. **LinkedIn is my recommended tool for connecting through social media, but Facebook and Twitter can be useful in building personal networks.** It is important to have complete and transparent online profiles complete with pictures, but don't use these tools passively. This book's chapter on LinkedIn offers specific tips and scripts on how to leverage this social media tool.

4. **Attend relevant speaking events, workshops, seminars or other social mixers to meet fellow profess-sionals.** Personally, I rarely attend these in the evening as there are ample opportunities for breakfast or lunchtime meetings. Consider hosting or co-hosting events at your

office or another venue. Organizing small gathering with interesting speakers on relevant topics allows you to play host and invite other business leaders you might not otherwise meet.

5. **Volunteer and get involved in the community.** Where is your passion? What causes excite you? Getting involved, first and foremost, should be about helping others. But, volunteering your time or serving on non-profit boards are excellent ways to meet like-minded professionals. Jo Ann Herold, Chief Marketing Officer of Interface and past-president of the Atlanta Chapter of the American Marketing Association shares this insight: "Networking and volunteering have always been important in my career. I like to join organizations I am passionate about, and I abide by the old saying: The more you give, the more you receive. I try to take a leadership role when I volunteer because it's a great way to get to know the organization, the members and the people we serve."

Helpful Tip:

Integrate networking into other activities. Neighborhood swim meets, youth sports events, church social activities and community volunteering all can be fortuitous opportunities to meet other professionals.

I have found more success in these casual settings than through any other avenue. There is something authentic about connecting initially as parents, through shared interests before discussing professional backgrounds. It builds trust which often leads to a mutually beneficial relationship.

The Payoff

Is investing time and energy in building a viable network worth it? Is there a pot of gold at the end of this rainbow? The answer is an emphatic "yes!" Professionals who are skilled at networking have access to people, resources and information to help solve problems and create opportunities. It encourages personal growth, benefits organizations and positively impacts the community. A strong network will also likely help you find your next job.

Although there are certainly more, here are five positive results of establishing and growing a dynamic network:

1. **If you are searching for a job, your network will help you.** As company loyalty to employees is declining, it is likely a professional will experience a transition at some point in his or her career. You owe it to yourself and to your family to prepare for that eventuality.

2. **Personal development and coaching will keep you active and engaged.** Most professionals I know believe development and coaching are lacking in organizations today. A dynamic network gives you access to new ideas, current trends and an ongoing opportunity to engage with a group of peers.

3. **Get ahead of the pending war for talent.** Don't be discouraged by high unemployment numbers and the myth that the streets are filled with top performers. The looming retirement of Baby Boomers and growing dissatisfaction among employees who have survived a tough economy (and are looking for new jobs) means there is a growing need to find good people quickly. Stay connected within your industry, know the players, and develop trusted networking resources to help find the best position. You may be unemployed now, but one day you will appreciate having access to talented people who can help you in a future job.

4. **You can do immense good in the community.** Investing time in getting your connections to support your causes (and in return support theirs) is a great way to exponentially leverage positive influence to serve the needs of others. Dr. Ron Young, president of Trove, shares this insight: "We should give of our time because it is the right thing to do. It feels good to be needed, we will be recharged and replenished far more than we give, and we will ultimately receive a return that is much larger than our investment."

5. **You can help your contacts with their business and career needs if you are highly networked.** Connecting others to new jobs and positive business relationships is an immensely gratifying act. Your willingness to help others will be reciprocated in your time of need.

Helpful Tip:

An important underlying theme of effective networking – *pay it forward.* Make your efforts about helping others and serving their needs and you will find networking to be a worthwhile, fulfilling experience. When it is all about you, people see your true intentions and networking becomes a miserable, laborious experience on many levels.

My networking endeavors have become a ritual for me. I meet people at the La Madeleine restaurant near my office beginning at 7:00 a.m. for coffee up to four days a week, and most of my lunches are with clients, team members, friends and networking contacts. I have spent many years building and organizing my network and am proud of the highly synergistic relationships we have developed to help our respective businesses, the community and each other.

Randy Patterson, a senior HR executive and committed networker offers this concluding insight: "Making the personal commitment to truly building and cultivating my network has been one of the best decisions of my life. In addition to building knowledge to solve business problems or helping me to find great talent for my organization, networking has introduced me to many friends who I will keep for the rest of my life."

Questions for Reflection:

1. Is my network viable and helpful? If not, am I willing to follow the direction from this chapter to grow it?
2. Are my networking efforts mostly done through email and LinkedIn, or am I intentionally pursuing face-to-face meetings whenever possible?
3. Do I maximize my personal and family life as another way to meet helpful people?

4. This chapter stresses the need to pay it forward as I build my network. Do I lead conversations by asking for what I want, or do I genuinely inquire about the other person's needs? Do I go out of my way to help them even though I am in need of a new job?

Action Item:

Take an honest inventory of your network and how you spend your time in a typical week. Use the methods shared in this chapter to grow the number of your contacts and connections, and spend more time getting to know them. Set an achievable goal each week for meeting new people and maintaining existing relationships.

5 NETWORKING WITH INTENTION

The exit process with your former employer is now complete and you are ready to find a wonderful new job elsewhere ... and fast. As you seek out a new role, it's important to keep in mind that what were considered to be traditional methods of job search, even just five or so years ago, are now largely obsolete.

Typically, most jobs applied for online fail to generate a response, most positions of interest are rarely made public, and I assure you it is highly unusual for someone to call out of the blue with a great opportunity. There has been a significant paradigm shift in job search that favors skilled networkers and relationship developers.

Here are the **Best Practices** for networking with intent to identify viable job opportunities. This is an amalgam of my experience with helpful feedback from hundreds of candidates over the years:

- Be intentional and don't waste time. You should be networking with people who can give you valuable job search assistance.

- Thank everyone and remember every kindness. Be professional and follow up every meeting with a handwritten note, or at least a "thank you" email.

- Have professional business cards made. They're inexpensive and very important when networking.

- Find an accountability partner to push you. Ask a friend, your spouse or someone else you trust to hold you accountable in your search. Check in with them frequently and ask them for candid feedback on how you are doing. This process is difficult to do by yourself.

- Remember the importance of metrics. A very effective way to measure your progress is through the number of meetings you've conducted. I suggest having at least four meetings a week with people who can provide assistance with your job search. This is more useful than email blasts and mass mailing your resume.

- Contact the Alumni Office of the schools you attended and ask for access to the alumni directory. This is often found online and can be a fantastic resource of professionals willing to help you.

- Join LinkedIn, build your profile and pay for the upgrade to have full access to the tools and features on the site. Because if its effectiveness, the next chapter of this book is devoted exclusively to useful ways you can utilize LinkedIn in a job search. The key is to connect directly with hiring managers and useful contacts. There are some benefits to Twitter and Facebook, but LinkedIn is specifically designed for business use and is the most widely used platform by professionals.

- Ask the senior executives of your former company(s) for referrals and active introductions to potential hiring managers in their network.

- Give your network a very clear request when asking for help: "I would be grateful for an active introduction to _____ in your network. Would you please introduce me via email and send them my resume?" This is so much more effective than the more common: "Keep me in mind if you hear of anything." The latter will not yield meaningful results.

- Never begin a conversation with a new networking contact like this: "I am in a job search. Can you help me?" Instead, offer assistance first. Make it about them and their needs, not just what you want. You could say, "I would like to explore ways we can help each other," or, "I would be glad to make my network available to you and would be grateful for any networking help you can provide me." Starting with the former initiates defensive behaviors and up goes the invisible wall.

- Become more active in the community. Aside from being the right thing to do, volunteering your time to non-profits and charities will provide you important exposure to other like-minded business people. Fair warning – be sincere and remember the importance of giving back to others. Real stewardship can't be faked.

- Consider joining networking groups, but be selective. There are useful groups, but unfortunately many are a waste of time. Make sure the ones you select are relevant to you, have interesting speakers and offer the potential of viable job leads and good networking contacts.

- Get connected to reputable search firms. Remember, search firms work for client companies to find candidates for their open positions. There is a common misconception that search firms are in the business of finding people jobs. It is always good to be referred to key players in a firm, which enhances your profile and credibility. Do your homework and ask around ... you will quickly see which firms are ethical and relationship focused. Key point: search firms want to help you, but outside of job search coaching, they are often limited in the help they can provide by the types of searches they are working on.

- Connect through content. Share relevant, informative articles with your network and potential hiring managers to demonstrate an interest in their business. It shows you are staying current. Even better, consider making a gift to a potential hiring manager of a book that has made an impact on you and include a handwritten note.

- Develop an "elevator pitch" about your background and what you are seeking. You should be able to share in less than 60 seconds your measurable accomplishments and what you are looking for in a new opportunity.

- Attend seminars, workshops or conferences relevant to your industry to stay current and visible.

Helpful Tip:

When networking and asking for assistance, be very specific about the kind of help you need. For example, "Bob, can you introduce me via email to the vice president of HR at your company and share my resume?"

Seeking more insight on the subject of effective networking, I reached out to Allen McNeill, a Vice President at Challenger, Gray & Christmas, Inc., who has been with the firm since 1999. The company provides job search support for departing executives and managers when their former organizations provide outplacement as a part of their severance package. I have known Allen for years and he is one of the best-networked individuals I have ever encountered.

Allen, in your role you spend a great deal of time with professionals in career transition. What advice would you share with them on the necessity of maintaining a strong network?

"When professionals lose or leave a job, they generally start off two to three months behind in the process of achieving their reemployment goals, and for one reason. They haven't developed or maintained their networks while employed. It does not take a lot of time, just a plan, to maintain relationships with acquaintances in all the sectors of our lives. I think LinkedIn is a wonderful tool to keep your network strong, up-to-date and viable if you are actively connecting with folks there."

Do you find the lack of a viable network is one of the biggest challenges job seekers have when they start seeking a new position?

"Jobs in today's market at the manager level and above are most often found through personal contacts and connections. It is not your contacts who provide the actual job, but the introductions to people they know who are connected to the company which has a job opening. In order to obtain a position, you must get a chance to tell your story. Your network and their contacts is the best way to increase the chances of telling your story to someone at the company you are targeting. Just sending in an application along with a resume is like a 'Hail Mary' pass – most are not successful."

What advice do you have for someone who is uncomfortable with networking? How can they overcome this common barrier to success?

"Networking is like selling. When I first started selling many years ago, I intensely disliked calling people on the phone. So I would start each day calling a friend and talking for a few minutes. This would get me comfortable on the phone so I was ready to call people who did not know me well or at all.

"Start the same way with networking. Meet first with people you know well. Get them to help introduce you to people they know so you have a warm call to make. A favorite technique of mine is to have someone make a virtual email introduction so that it is a nonthreatening environment for the parties needing to connect. The two people introduced can then email and get comfortable with one another before meeting.

"Networking to me is best as a one-on-one meeting, not small or large group gatherings. But if you find yourself on occasion attending a group networking event for job seekers, go with three goals in mind:

1. You are there to help others. If that is not your first priority, then do not go.
2. A job search is very personal and each person must develop his or her own style. Relax and be yourself in these settings.
3. Set out to meet 2-3 people (you don't have to connect with the entire room) that you want to know or help in some way. Schedule a one-on-one meeting with each of them to

find how you can help each other. This is valuable networking."

I acknowledging that not everyone is comfortable with the necessity of networking, and some even find the process to be somewhat dreadful. The key is to make the way you network fit your personality and style – beyond these fairly intuitive suggestions, there isn't one roadmap for how to do it. Make it your own and you will feel most at ease. For example, I love coffee meetings and strongly prefer one-on-one discussions versus large events with a room full of people. Do whatever you must to reduce the anxiety around networking and make your comfort level a priority because networking is such a critical part of the job search process.

Questions for Reflection:

1. Is my approach to networking effective in opening doors for me? Is what I am doing producing other desired results?
2. Do I know my networking style? Am I maximizing my networking time by doing what is most comfortable for me?
3. If I am honest with myself, how do I think others I am reaching out to and networking with perceive me? What can I change about my approach to get people interested and even excited about helping me in my search?
4. Am I clear in what I am asking of others when I network, based on the advice in this chapter? If not, what can I do to make sure the other person knows exactly what I am requesting?

Action Item:

Starting now, write down the next 10 interactions you have with people you reach through networking or ask for networking assistance. Write a few notes about each interaction and how close this interaction gets you to a viable job opportunity. If you are not getting closer to that end result, it is time to make changes.

6 PRACTICAL LINKEDIN

Without a doubt, the best tool for connecting business people is LinkedIn. It focuses on connecting business professionals and doesn't bore you with the minutiae of Twitter or the more social, casual focus of Facebook – although both are gaining popularity among recruiters to find candidates. Also, it is clear that how we build personal and business connections is ever evolving.

Despite the rising popularity of new social media tools, LinkedIn has enjoyed rapid growth. A recent search of their website revealed that as of the publishing of this book, LinkedIn has more than 238 million members in more than 200 countries, and is adding new ones at the rate of two new members per second.

Consider these statistics:

- All 500 of the Fortune 500 are represented on LinkedIn. In fact, all of them are represented by director-level and above employees.
- More than 1.4 million members self-identify as senior executives.
- Most members tend to be between 30 and 55-years-old.
- More than 2 million companies have LinkedIn pages.

For the purpose of this chapter, I make two basic assumptions: you are 1) familiar with LinkedIn and 2) interested in expanding your network for personal or professional reasons. With these assumptions in mind, let's explore different ways to approach LinkedIn, paradigm shifts among users of the site and best/worst practices.

"I have a profile, now what do I do?" This is the question I hear most often. Whether you are a job seeker, sales professional, recruiter, or you are simply interested in making new connections, you will see best results by approaching LinkedIn with this mindset:

1. **Have a "pay it forward" attitude.** Be open and willing to actively accept invitations and help people connect to your network.

2. **Focus on finding people you don't know.** This seems obvious, but it can be easy to fall into the habit of "collecting" contacts you already know. I find the real value of LinkedIn is connecting with people of different backgrounds and capabilities outside of your current network who can help you with your objective.

3. **Reach out to those people you don't know.** A majority of people on LinkedIn are open to networking, so don't be afraid to introduce yourself. Networking is likely why they joined in the first place.

4. **View LinkedIn as an enormous spider web.** Your direct connections and their connections and their connection's connections are all part of your network. So, get as many direct contacts as possible to ensure that you can run searches within a very large population.

5. **Be transparent in your profile and complete it fully.** Add a professional headshot in your profile. Give clear descriptions of the jobs you've had and always include a bio under the Summary section. Also, I advocate sharing personal interests, charitable causes you support, hobbies, affinity and social groups, faith, etc. We will review why this is important later.

6. **Recognize that managing your online presence is critically important.** In the age of search engines, social

media and Big Data, it is practically impossible to hide work and personal Information if you conduct any personal or professional business online. Utilize LinkedIn to showcase the information you want to share. With the typically high placement of LinkedIn profiles in search engine returns, you are likely to have this seen first by others.

7. **Don't let LinkedIn serve as a substitute for human interaction.** Any people-oriented business thrives on relationships and face-to-face meetings. Utilize this tool to make the connection and build a bridge, but always follow up with a phone call and a meeting.

These approaches to working with and maximizing what LinkedIn offers have served me well. And my technique continues to evolve as my needs change and the technology becomes more sophisticated.

I am always keenly interested in how different people use LinkedIn, and I routinely ask clients, candidates, friends and peers for their perspectives. The results may surprise you. Here is what I have learned over the last few years:

- Most of my clients look at a candidate's profile on LinkedIn before he or she comes in for an interview. Their intent is to gain insight into the more personal side of the candidate, as well as to check for resume inconsistencies. Don't let this scare you and use it to your advantage. Sharing the right personal information may give you the edge you need to land the position.

- Most of my friends in professional services utilize LinkedIn to research their client prospects and gain a competitive advantage by being well informed. The ability to discuss different aspects of a person's professional and personal history adds depth and distinctiveness to the conversation. Candidates often do the same with prospective employers.

- LinkedIn has become an excellent way to build a personal brand. Be deliberate in how you use this channel to market yourself and your particular areas of expertise. To drive more traffic to your LinkedIn profile, consider adding a link at the bottom of your email signature that goes directly to your page.

- Corporate recruiters and executive search firms, including my own, have realized over the last few years that LinkedIn is a rich source of high-quality candidates and use it as a primary recruiting source.

- Corporate leaders are frequently looking at their own employee profiles to learn personal information for a variety of reasons. They also look to see if current employees are job hunting, so use caution when checking the box that says you are interested in "Career Opportunities." You may also want to change your personal settings to stop sharing these types of profile updates with your network.

- LinkedIn is a great channel for sharing content – your own writing, the blog posts/articles of others, interesting news stories, etc. This will indicate your desire to stay relevant and show you have a deep knowledge of the trends in your industry.

- LinkedIn User Groups are exploding in popularity and are transforming into "mini-communities" of like-minded users with shared interests. Share a link to an interesting article you come across here too since engaging others will often encourage them reciprocate.

There are constantly changes in this as well as any online and social medium, but these are the shifts I'm seeing most frequently related to a job search. Just to reiterate, there are no secrets on the Internet, and you have complete control over the content you share on LinkedIn. Simply exercise good judgment.

In general, aren't we interested in learning a better way of doing things? Adopt that strategy with LinkedIn. No one has all the answers, so an open mind and willingness to innovate will serve you well as you turn LinkedIn into an effective tool.

As I've spoken and presented ideas on LinkedIn for the job search to audiences of all types over the years, I always get positive feedback on my best and worst practices, so I'm sharing them here. **First, the Best Practices:**

- **Log on to LinkedIn daily**, especially your home page to track movement in your network that may benefit you – job changes, promotions, new connections, etc. Because LinkedIn is an active site with continual updates, it is a good idea to keep an eye out for new names/companies that may be of value to you. You can also see if anyone from your school(s) has joined LinkedIn and look at the people who have viewed your profile recently. If you don't have time to look each day, you can have a daily or weekly recap of all activity in your network sent to you via email from LinkedIn.

- **Upgrade your account.** The entry (free) level of LinkedIn is tedious if you are using it to make a large number of connections. Pay for at least the first upgrade level so you can connect to people in your network directly through InMail, rather than waiting weeks for a referral.

- **Have a transparent profile that will attract broad interest.** You are screening in, not screening out, and it is important to connect with as many people as possible in your network. A broader sharing of your background is likely to gain more contacts and allow you to connect with others with similar backgrounds. Also, list personal and business accomplishments that will help showcase your achievements and interests.

- **Post your picture on your profile.** Your picture humanizes the connecting process and facilitates relationship building. I always tell people, "I have a face made for radio, and if I can put my picture on there, so can you."

- **Have several recommendations on your pro-file.** Recommendations are analogous to a "Good Seller" rating on eBay – you are viewed as credible and more likely to get a call back if a viewer sees that people think highly of you. Recommending people in your network will prompt them to recommend you in return. This is a good "pay it forward" strategy. Also, you can endorse others' skills listed on their profiles. It is a good idea to do this from time to time as the gesture will usually be returned in kind by the recipient.

- **When searching for people, run Boolean searches for prospects by using keywords relevant to your background.** Place quotation marks around more than two words in a search in order to keep them together. My examples include: "University of Georgia," "Boy Scouts" and "Catholic Church." Otherwise, the search will be too broad and not helpful. Search any keywords relevant and important to you that will help build a connection to someone who shares these descriptors in their profile. Keep playing with keywords and companies you are interested in until you find people you would like to meet. This is what I call affinity-based connecting.

- **Focus on contacts who can help you get to the right person.** If you spend time searching for the perfect job-related decision maker, you'll only be disappointed. It's not likely that you will be successful. Instead, look for people in the target organization who share common interests, schools or LinkedIn connections with you. It's much more effective than a cold call since the natural connection may open the door to a friendly introduction to the right person. However, if you can't establish common ground with someone at a target company, the cold contact may be necessary.

- **Always offer to help someone before asking for help.** When reaching out via InMail (assuming you now have the upgraded LinkedIn account), never state your desire or need in the opening sentence. I've had success with this approach: "John: I came across your background on LinkedIn and noticed that we both are UGA alums and involved in Boy Scouts. I run an executive search firm here in Atlanta and am always looking to grow my network. Would you be open to a call this week and perhaps a cup of coffee? I would like to see if there are ways I can help you and maybe we can share stories of our college days! You can check out my firm at www.belloaks.com and I can be reached directly at _____. I look forward to hearing from you. Thanks, Randy Hain." I've included a list of other scripts at the end of this chapter that may be helpful.

- **Invite every person you meet to join your network.** This helps build your list of direct connections and expands your searchable pool of contacts. Mention when you meet that you will connect with them on LinkedIn to increase your chance of an accepted invitation.

- **Join groups to enhance your searches and help you be strategically identified.** You can join affinity groups on LinkedIn in almost every category ranging from alumni associations to industry sectors and specialty areas to personal interests. Groups have become well-defined communities where you can easily gain new connections, engage in discussions, and become a noted expert.

- **Start your own User Group on LinkedIn.** If you have a business, non-profit or group you would like to promote, this is an effective method. As the Group "owner" you will load a logo, mission/purpose statement and invite people to join. You will also be able to moderate very useful discussions and share news of interest to the members.

- **Utilize the Update box feature at the top of your profile.** This is a great way to let your network know what you are working on, or to share links to great articles and interesting news. Remember, you want to stay in front of people in your network without always asking for something and this is a great way to do it – sharing ideas.

- **Publicize your work.** LinkedIn offers several ways you can link to your articles and presentations and publicize them on your profile. Take advantage of this great opportunity to show off your work.

So let's move on to some equally important **Worst Practices** that we can all learn from.

- **Join LinkedIn, develop a profile and don't accept new contacts or requests for help.** Why go through the trouble if you are not going to use it? LinkedIn won't put you on a secret "bad" list, but don't waste your time if you aren't committed to utilizing the tool. Also, if the tables are turned one day and you are looking for some help, these people will remember your non-answer to their connection invitation.

- **Abuse your network.** Be careful not to go to the same people again and again for referrals. They should be open to the request, but too many requests will create negative response to your interactions and may possibly burn a bridge.

- **Send invitations to people you don't know without a personal message or explanation of why you wish to connect.** This is an enormous problem on LinkedIn and so prolific. It makes the person sending the invitation look unprofessional. These are the invitations I rarely accept.

- **Be afraid to reach out to people you don't know.** This is a common stumbling block. Remember that LinkedIn users are generally open to referral requests and direct contact. Direct connections to people with whom you share something in common with will accelerate your business development, recruiting or connecting efforts exponentially.

- **I don't want my information "out there" on the Internet, so I won't share much.** As I mentioned earlier in this chapter, like it or not, you're already "out there." Google yourself and if you are a business professional with any experience, you will probably show up. Share your career information and use discretion when including personal information if you prefer (birthdate, residence, etc.). This is the direction technology has taken us, so I encourage you to leverage it.

- **Don't share access to your connections.** If you plan to ask others for access to their connections, you must be willing to share yours. Some people do use LinkedIn as a master contact manager, but I argue that part of the value of the network is open and transparent sharing of information and referrals. If someone you don't know or trust asks for a referral to one of your connections, simply say no.

- **Don't fill out your profile completely.** You can't make LinkedIn work for you unless you have a profile that legitimizes you as a credible professional. I see many half-completed profiles and I wonder how many opportunities they miss.

- **Treat LinkedIn like Twitter and Facebook.** Please don't share the boring or highly personal minutiae often seen on Twitter or Facebook. Also, don't post a potentially embarrassing casual photo of yourself, or anything else, on your profile that would shed an unfavorable light on your professional image.

There are literally thousands of articles out there on how to best capitalize on LinkedIn, so I certainly don't profess to have all the answers. Most of what I do on LinkedIn has been self-taught through experimentation, observing others' best practices and logically evaluating what works best. Our firm has generated 20-25% percent of our revenue from LinkedIn client and candidate sources over the last five years. Clearly, there can be a significant ROI in utilizing LinkedIn effectively.

To add an additional perspective, I sought the experience of recent job seeker, Michael Thomas, who used LinkedIn to land a new job. Michael hails from South Bend, IN and attended the University of Dayton, where he studied finance and marketing. He spent the past two years working for GE on their Financial Management Program, supporting business goals and objectives and learning about different businesses within their Energy portfolio. He now works for a global Fortune 50 company on the finance team in their mobile device division.

Michael, I recognize from our past conversations that LinkedIn was not always a big part of your networking strategy. What changed?

"Before my job search, I always thought of LinkedIn as a 'check the box' tool that everyone in the professional world has. I didn't realize how useful it actually is. After a year or so into my first job, I realized that this career path wasn't right for me personally, and I started reaching out to a number of different people on LinkedIn. This is when I started to realize the functionality of it and how useful it is in networking and overall job search. The reality is that most people, even those you've only met once or twice, are extremely willing to help and would be more than happy to make introductions. The more you use LinkedIn as a tool to grow your network, the wider you cast your net and the more potential there is for a valuable connection to be made."

You recently Landed a brand new job with a global Fortune 50 company. What role did LinkedIn play in your efforts to find the job and conduct research?

"LinkedIn played a very large role in the initial stages of my job search. First and foremost, it allowed me a very useful and intuitive way to research the company, see what job openings were posted, and determine who of my connections works for that company and who might be able to make introductions on my behalf.

"The insight that LinkedIn provides above and beyond specific company websites is tremendous. Company job postings are typically ambiguous and un-descriptive. Using LinkedIn, I was able to not only see what jobs were open for that company, but after I narrowed it down to a few roles, I could research who has held the same or a similar role in the past and what their background was. As a candidate, this gives valuable insight into whether you're actually a good fit for the job, or if you're wasting your time on a role for which you might be over- or under-qualified.

"Once I identified the roles that interested me and that fit my background/experience, I used LinkedIn to determine who in my network would be able to make an introduction on my behalf. I was then positioned to reach out individually and ask them to make an introduction, always offering to return the favor if the situation should ever come up. What makes LinkedIn so great is that it combines a company with its people, and adds a personal aspect that a job search site or company website cannot offer. It's a one-stop shop for articles, information and job openings for most companies, saving tremendous amount of time during the research stage of the job search."

As a member of Gen Y, do you think your generational peer group uses this tool effectively?

"I feel that Gen Y does a tremendous job of using LinkedIn as a job search tool, but I also think it could be used more effectively. In my experience, and that of many of my close friends, LinkedIn is the go-to tool to start the job search. We're in a digital age, and it makes sense that this digital tool is top of mind when it comes to professional networking.

"But the problem isn't whether the tool is used; it's how the tool is used. The primary benefit of LinkedIn is that it provides the opportunity to connect on a personal level with people who can help in your job search, which means reaching out to anyone with whom you have personal connections (college, religion, company, etc.). Most members of Gen Y don't do this, especially if they've not met them personally, which is a mistake. Whether it's fear of rejection or lack of perceived benefit, the fact is that most people don't access the incredible amount of information and potential connectivity at their fingertips."

What are the biggest mistakes you see people making on LinkedIn?

"Most users do not utilize the advanced search to its full extent to find valuable potential connections and reach out to them. This feature can be useful in finding people with similar backgrounds (university, current or former job) and interests (non-profit affiliations, specific project work) for which a user can reach out and use as the basis for an introduction. It can be uncomfortable at first to contact someone you've not met in person, but most are very willing to help and you never know who might be able to suggest a job or put you in contact with the right people."

Are there any valuable lessons about using LinkedIn that you would like to share?

"Give honest recommendations and endorsements – these mean a great deal to people and show that your interactions with them in the past meant something. To me, writing a thoughtful recommendation shows you're someone who pays attention to detail and cares enough to take the time to share your personal experiences. It is also likely that they will return the favor!"

View LinkedIn as an enormous network of potential new friends, but with a word of advice – don't let it become one of the omnipresent technological devices that make it so easy to hide behind. LinkedIn should be used as a catalyst, not a substitute, for human interaction and conversation.

Employ a "pay it forward" strategy of helping others through referrals and recommendations. Operate out of enlightened self-interest as you reach out to people and offer to help them first. Ask for what you want later, after rapport and common interests have been established. Use LinkedIn to promote your personal brand and develop your profile as a marketing showcase that will attract others. LinkedIn has become an effective networking tool for me and countless others and I hope it becomes the same for you.

Helpful Scripts

A sampling of script ideas for use on LinkedIn when reaching out via InMail.

One of the biggest challenges I hear from people about using LinkedIn is this: "What do I say when I reach out to people?" To help get you started, I have developed scripts to be used when communicating via InMail on LinkedIn. These have been tested and work effectively to solicit a response from whomever you are trying to reach.

Good afternoon. I came across your background on LinkedIn and noticed we have a few things in common, including our time at UGA and a shared interest in Habitat for Humanity. I would like to connect with you this week by phone to see if we might be able to help each other. What is the best way to reach you and what days can you chat for a few minutes?

Sincerely,
John Smith

Good morning. I noticed we are both members of the SHRM-Atlanta Group on LinkedIn. I am always interested in connecting with fellow HR professionals in the business world and would like to speak with you in the coming weeks if you are available. How can I reach you by phone?

Thank you,
Bill Johnson

_____-- good morning! I came across your background on LinkedIn today and noticed that we have a few friends in common. Also, I see we both worked for Home Depot at one time. I would welcome a chance to speak by phone this week. I am happy to make my network available to you and I would like to see if you could assist me with expanding my network. I look forward to hearing from you.

Thanks!
John Smith

Good morning, _____. My research and networking have pointed me towards an open position in your organization that appears to be a great fit. I would welcome an opportunity to speak with you, make a connection and hopefully schedule time to meet. I encourage you to look at my profile to gain an understanding of my background. How is the best way for me to reach you by phone this week?

Thanks in advance for your time.

Sincerely,
John Smith

_____-- hello. We haven't spoken in a while, but I hope all is well with you and your family. I noticed on LinkedIn that you are connected to Bill Thomas, VP of Sales at ABC company. I was recently downsized at my company and would be grateful for an active introduction to Bill. Would you be willing to help me connect with him? Are you up for a cup of coffee to catch up? Let me know what works for you.

Thanks in advance for your help.
John

Questions for Reflection

1. Based on the lessons in this chapter, have I maximized LinkedIn in my job search?
2. The author stresses the need to be authentic and transparent throughout this book. Am I prepared to share who I am and what is important to me on my LinkedIn profile? What are the potential consequences of not being transparent?
3. Does the approach Michael Thomas took resonate with me? Do I see the effectiveness of his LinkedIn experience? Can I make it work for me?
4. Do I have an effective script for reaching out to people I don't know on LinkedIn? Can I adapt the ones offered here?

Action Item:

This chapter is filled with very practical action items and ideas. Note in your journal what's been missing in regards to your LinkedIn activities and record your job search results so far. Make another list of the changes you are going to make based on these recommendations and see if any of them lead to success in finding your next job.

7 BEING INTENTIONAL ABOUT BUSINESS RELATIONSHIPS

Every action we take with regard to relationships in the business world is intentional. On some level, we know what we are doing, but may not always consider the impact of our actions or the repercussions. The challenge is, people on the receiving end take notice, and they are not likely to forget. We may be perceived as a "giver" or a "taker." Maybe they see us as either "artificial" or "authentic." Regardless, it is important to know how we come across to others and make corrections if necessary.

Most of my insight around relationships comes from observing job seekers in action and people responsible for business development within their organizations. Both categories of professionals rely on networks of people to achieve their goals. What has been obvious to me over the years is the clear demarcation between best and worst relationship practices. Here they are:

Worst Business Relationship Practices:

- Only reaching out when you need something.
- Only talking about yourself.
- Mistaking connections through social media as substitutes for real relationships.
- Avoiding being personal.

- Failing to be transparent about what you want.
- Going from "hello" with a new contact to "I want..." without building a trusting and open relationship first.
- Keeping score.
- Abusing your network with frequent requests.
- Not following up appropriately.
- Failing to show gratitude.

Best Business Relationship Practices:

- Being authentic.
- Getting personal. Your transparency will invite them to be transparent in return.
- Being candid.
- Always trying to "pay it forward" offering to help the other person first.
- Being insatiably curious about others. Learn and remember personal things like a spouse's and child's name, hobbies, interests and birthdays.
- Finding meaningful ways to touch base with your network consistently throughout the year.
- Freely sharing ideas, connections and content to add value to the relationship.
- Doing what you say you will do.
- Meeting people in person whenever it's convenient and appropriate.
- Always expressing gratitude.

I have certainly wrestled with being consistent in following the "Best Practices" list over the years, but each interaction with another professional has been a lesson-filled experience. That's helped me improve in this area so critical to achieving professional and personal success. Why did I feel compelled to include this part in the book? Unfortunately, I have observed countless business relationships get off to the wrong start or end in frustration and failure because of a stubborn pursuit of the actions on the "Worst Practices" list.

I suggest that a pervasive lack of self-awareness and an unbalanced focus on our own needs are the principal contributors to poorly held business relationships. If you feel convicted about your own relationship building practices and sincerely desire to change, I encourage you to do these three things:

1. Reflect on your last five encounters with people in your business network. What were the results? Be honest. What can you improve on? How many of your actions were on the worst list vs. the best list?
2. Ask the most honest and candid person you know to give you feedback on how you handle relationships. Don't seek encouragement or validation from this conversation. This exercise requires absolute honesty.
3. Ask for feedback from a "failed" business encounters. Be sincere in your request for thoughts on how they perceived you, and how you might have approached them differently. You may not always get a response (or like what you hear), but the lesson is invaluable.

If you are on the job hunt, looking to develop new business, or someone dependent on strong relationships, consider how intentional you have been in your past actions. Are you satisfied with your efforts and results to date? Think about times you have been on the receiving end of the Worst Relationship Practices. How did these encounters make you feel?

Dare to be different. Build a strong network of like-minded professionals and nurture these valuable relationships with a new mindset and approach. Be the opposite of every bad encounter you've ever had in business. I have always found that being friendly, curious, authentic and sincerely asking, "What can I do to help you?" has been the best way to get business relationships off to a great start.

What about other approaches to building relationships? I sought the input of a well-networked professional, Susan O'Dwyer, who I have known and admired for years. Susan is the Director of Business Development for one of the top public accounting firms in the Southeast. She is a selfless and caring leader who rarely misses an opportunity to meet with other professionals to see how she may be of service.

Susan, you are one of the most connected people I know and are frequently sought out by people in career transition. What is your advice to professionals looking to expand their networks and develop new relationships?

"To the person receiving the email, 'Hey, it's been a long time. Can I buy you a cup of coffee?', this is code for, 'I'm unemployed and need help finding my next job.' And it feels like you are being used.

"People in transition often wait to connect with people until they need help. They have allowed themselves to be consumed by their job, travel and other priorities, and not nurtured their relationships along the way. When these bonds wither and die, not only are they difficult to resurrect, you lose access to people who really know you and could speak to your talents and skills as a credible reference. My advice is to focus on actively connecting with your contacts, continuously and regularly, particularly when you don't 'need' something from them."

We have discussed before that networking and building relationships is challenging for many professionals. Why is this so difficult?

"Professionals find relationship building challenging is because their focus is misplaced. Most will tell you that they 'hate' networking because they don't know what to say, so they usually talk about what they are most comfortable with – themselves. Not that many people, outside of your parents and spouse, are honestly that interested in you. Instead, turn the conversation around to asking questions about the other person because you are genuinely interested. It is very easy to get people to talk and tell you all sorts of things that help you understand *their* interests, passions and challenges, which makes it much easier to be of service and build an earnest relationship."

What common mistakes you have observed with networking over your career?

"There are three I see on a frequent basis:

1. Not being an active listener instead focusing on yourself. If they inquire how you are, keep it short and generally positive without launching into a therapy session.

2. Not looking for ways to be of service – connecting the other person with a potential client, sending a helpful link or article that may be of interest, etc. It is extremely rare for people to follow up, but when they do, it is noteworthy and memorable.

3. Not knowing who your target professionals are when you attend a networking meeting. Do your homework ahead of time and think about who you want to meet and why. If you don't know them, learn who in your network could introduce you."

Thank you, Susan. There are common themes here that both Susan O'Dwyer and I are suggesting in regards to building effective business relationships: Be real. Pay it forward. Don't make it all about you. Be a good listener. Do your research.

It is time to take stock. How are you doing with your business relationships?

Questions for Reflection:

1. The themes of authenticity and "pay it forward" are clear in this chapter. Have I been authentic and focused on the needs of others during my job search? Is this difficult for me? Why or why not?
2. The Worst Practices List is very convincing. How many of these have I been doing? What can I do to make the necessary changes?
3. Susan O'Dwyer refers to "being used" in her answer to the first question. Is it possible people in my network feel used by me during my job search?
4. Do I have a good grasp on how I am being perceived by others as I conduct my job search? Is there anyone in my circle who I can depend on to give me candid feedback?

Action Item:

Take a thorough, honest look at your relationship building practices to date. Be frank with yourself and list the "worst" as well as the "best" efforts you have made during your job search. Apply the guidance given in this chapter to revive previous relationships that may have faded away and record your progress.

8 ASKING OUR FRIENDS & NETWORK FOR HELP

Our close friends, if they know we are in need, want to help. Our network, if approached correctly, is likely to assist. However, the problem is that we may be approaching the people we need the most with poor information, unclear objectives and sloppy follow-up. Let me explain.

One of the most common phrases I hear from a job seeker is this: "Keep me in mind if you hear of anything that fits my background." This seems logical, but it is very ineffective. The person you are sharing this with will keep you in mind until they get busy with other priorities, and then you slide down the list of what is important. This can be rectified with a more direct approach:

"Jim, thank you for meeting with me. May I ask you for a favor? I noticed on LinkedIn that you are connected to the head of Human Resources for ABC company. If I send you an email asking for an introduction with my resume, would you mind forwarding the message on to her along with a personal recommendation? There is a position open in their sales organization that looks like a great fit for my background. I am grateful for your help."

This request is specific and clear. There is no guesswork. You are doing most of the work and all Jim needs to do is forward an email, if they are willing, to someone in their network. The results are much more likely to be positive with this type of approach.

Here are additional helpful actions to consider when meeting a friend or network contact about your job search:

1. If you are not already connected via LinkedIn, ask for permission to invite the person to join your network. Also, if they have made a sincere offer to help you, ask if you can review their LinkedIn network for useful connections.
2. Develop a target list of specific companies (not industries) you are interested in and ask if you can email them this information.
3. If you are meeting a busy and connected person who keeps dropping useful names into the conversation, ask if they happen to have the email addresses and phone numbers of these individuals on their smartphone (most people will). Offer to reach out directly to these useful contacts and copy the person you are meeting on the email. This may seem bold, but for busy people like me, it is a great time saver and you have taken responsibility for a huge follow-up step.
4. Offer to follow up with the other person on any action items in your discussion as well keeping them updated on the progress of your search.
5. Always show gratitude!
6. Always offer to reciprocate. Ask the friend/network contact if you can send a short email recapping the meeting with your resume attached. Again, offer to send them a list of your target companies in a separate email. Ask if they would be willing to forward the email/resume on to helpful people in their network with a recommendation for a meeting. Again, this is a huge time saver for people you are asking for help.

Here's an example:

Bill,

Thank you for meeting with me today. I really enjoyed our conversation and appreciate your willingness to help me grow my network. As we discussed, I am looking for a senior sales leadership role in a growing technology company. I have a long track record of success in my past roles and will bring leadership experience, a great reputation and a wealth of contacts to a new position. Again, I am grateful for your assistance and I look forward to speaking with you again soon.

Sincerely,
Mike Smith

Have you noticed that in most of these examples, *you* are taking responsibility for a specific follow-up item? This is important because you're asking this individual for help, so you should make it as simple and easy as possible. This approach is more efficient, contains more accountability and ultimately gets you what you desire – "warm" contacts from your friends and network.

Seeking another voice on this topic, I reached out to Jodi Weintraub. Jodi is a well-respected Market Lead for TrueBridge Resources, the professional staffing division of North Highland. She has more than 25 years of experience in executive HR and professional staffing leadership roles, and has worked in startups to the Fortune 100.

Jodi, one of the reasons I was excited to interview you is because I know you meet with professionals in career transition on a regular basis and have developed approaches and strategies to help them. Can you share your thoughts on the quality of the networks you typically see from job seekers?

"In general, I'm usually a little disappointed at the quality, particularly from those folks who have been in the market 20+ years and should have a broader network. Many of people I meet with view networking as something to do when they are in a job search, not something that you do to stay relevant in the business community in general. Networking is a thoughtful, deliberate approach to making sure you are a vibrant and contributing member of your extended community. If you wait to connect with people until you need something from them, I think you are missing a great opportunity to grow both personally and professionally."

Do you think job seekers do a good job of maximizing their networks and enlisting their friends to help?

"I think many people miss the boat when it comes to enlisting their friends and personal networks during the job search process. My gut tells me they are embarrassed to have to ask for help, when in reality I think most people want to help, they just don't necessarily know how. It's really up to the job seeker to frame their request in a way that makes it easy for the friend to help. Asking someone if he knows about any job openings puts that person in an awkward position if he has to say 'no.'

"Think about all the ways that you can leverage another person's existing networks: Can they connect you with someone who can help you understand an industry better? Can they connect you with someone who is currently employed at a particular company you are interested in? Can they introduce you to one of the vendors they work with? There are so many ways to leverage relationships – use the account management approach of relationship mapping to see where it can take you. Make it easy for your friends to help you."

What are practical ways job seekers can overcome reluctance or awkwardness when seeking help? Are there best practices?

"I don't know of a 'best practices' approach, but I do have some suggestions I think might help. Ask people open-ended questions – if someone only has to give a yes or no response to your questions, it can be difficult to engage them in a sustained conversation. Make sure you are direct with people about what you are looking for – don't ask them to figure out your career path for you. Help them understand why it makes sense for them to make an introduction for you, and offer to write an email that they can forward on to someone. And make sure to follow up with a thank you note – it makes a big difference. Finally, don't forget to send them a note when you do land your job, and offer to help them in any way you can."

For you personally, what actions can someone in transition take to get you energized and excited about assisting them with their job search?

"To me, nothing is more important than doing your homework before you meet with me. Don't give me a list of 50 companies you found on a list somewhere and ask me if I know of any contacts there. Make sure I understand what you are looking for, and why you think you would be a good fit at a particular company. Don't expect me to just open up my Rolodex (or LinkedIn contacts) to you – I've worked hard to build and maintain my own network, and I don't want to risk it on someone I don't think will be respectful of it. Help me figure out how to position you when I present you to someone I know. Make it easy for me to help you."

Smart advice from Jodi. If you are stuck in your job search and wondering why, reflect on how you have interacted with your friends and network. Ask yourself if you have followed the ideas outlined in this chapter, or how you can improve at providing your best job search resources with the right information and clear objectives. This is a common problem, but one that is easily rectified.

Questions for Reflection:

1. As I consider my last five networking meetings, have I followed the advice in this chapter? If I am honest with myself, can I improve my results?
2. Do I feel comfortable being as direct with my friends and network as the author and Jodi Weintraub are suggesting? If not, what do I find challenging and how can I overcome it?
3. Do I know how to articulate what I want? Am I clear enough to provide my friends and network what they require to truly help me?
4. The importance of gratitude was mentioned in this chapter. Have I shown sincere gratitude to my friends and network?

Action Item:

Prepare carefully for your next meeting with a friend or someone from your network by following all of the guidance in this chapter. Make note of the results and keep practicing this approach in future meetings until you routinely see fruit from your efforts.

SECTION III

RESUMES, INTERVIEWING & NEGOTIATING

9 NOT OVERTHINKING RESUMES

In all my years of business, rarely have I observed anything that generates as much anxiety for candidates as the state of their resumes. There seems to be a general belief that a perfect resume (is there such a thing?) will help them land the perfect job. Nothing could be further from the truth.

My hope in this chapter is to recalibrate your thinking about resumes and ask you to simply focus on preparing a quality resume as part of the overall job search process. Placing too much emphasis on resume preparation can distract you from the more important issues of the job search process that we have been discussing in this book.

I have long shared with candidates my belief that a well-done resume should accomplish at least the following six objectives:

1. Spark enough interest from the hiring manager or resume screener to schedule an interview. There is a general belief that hiring managers rarely read more than the first third of a resume and briefly scan the rest. My informal surveys of clients over the years make me believe this is accurate, so create a memorable resume from the beginning.
2. Have a clear objective (what are you seeking?) and chronological job history with specific accomplishments (no fluff or overuse of adjectives). The resume should not

exceed two pages in length, so don't write the same thing over and over again.

3. Your resume should be free of grammatical errors, formatting problems, use of slang or other information that could reflect poorly on your candidacy and professionalism.

4. Impress a hiring manager with your experiences and clear message. Do not attempt to impress them with tired and overused buzzwords such as "innovative", "strategic", "creative" and "team player." Find alternatives that mean the same thing, but allow you to distinguish your resume from others.

5. Remember, numbers speak louder than words. Don't say, "I was part of a sales team that exceeded our annual goal," if you can honestly say, "I played a key leadership role on our five-person sales team in exceeding our 2012 revenue goal by 23%."

6. Whenever possible, tailor your Objective Statement to reflect the job description of the role for which you are interviewing. This will help your resume stand out to a hiring manager over the ubiquitous fill-in-the-blank type resumes.

There are numerous professional resume writers available who can help you develop a quality resume for a fee (under $500 is considered reasonable). But, be leery of resume services promising you will find a great job because of their efforts. An exorbitant fee is typically attached to their services, and I have never heard of anyone receiving the full return on this investment.

Before engaging a professional resume firm, try downloading resume templates from the Internet to serve as an example to follow. Also, please avoid working with firms who promise to send your resume to a large number of hiring managers or boldly guarantee they will find you a job. In my experience, I have never encountered a professional who has found a new job this way.

Seeking additional input from an HR professional who has also viewed countless resumes and interviewed hundreds of candidates over his career, I interviewed experienced senior human resources leader, Russ Wise, who is based in Atlanta.

Russ, as a senior HR leader with extensive large company experience, you have likely reviewed thousands of resumes. In your opinion, what is the true value of a resume?

"Resumes have staying power and are still the optimum way to present a candidate's credentials. While social media sites, such as LinkedIn, have provided additional tools, the resume continues to be an important method for candidates to succinctly organize their relevant credentials, accomplishments and job objectives to perspective employers."

How do hiring managers in your current company, as well as past employers, view resumes? What are they looking for? What really grabs their attention?

"A resume review focuses on the necessary requirements in terms of education, skills and technical requirements and relevant work history. Candidates with industry experience will stand out to our hiring managers, as well as specifics on how they delivered value to their employer and internal/external customers. Numbers-oriented resumes with measurable results really set a candidate apart."

Do you have a do's and don'ts list for candidate resumes?
"From my perspective, there are some pretty clear do's and don'ts when it comes to building a stellar resume.

Here are some for the **Do** list:

- Keep it clean, simple, brief and factual. In your overview, be clear on the type of opportunity you are looking for and what you bring to the table.
- Provide a brief timeline of previous positions held and list key accomplishments in how you delivered value.
- Provide more information on recent positions than earlier positions since what you've done most recently is more relevant experience.
- Make sure the information on your resume is up to date and consistent with your LinkedIn profile and other sites.

- Include information on relevant professional and community association involvement to portray a more rounded profile.

And this is my **Don'ts** list for resumes:

- Have your resume read like a job description.
- Stray from the truth or omit information that could raise suspicion.
- Get fancy with fonts or paper. This only creates distraction.
- Overwhelm the reader with too much content."

Resumes are an important tool, but they are not the critical driver of your job search. Follow the advice in this chapter, hire a professional resume writer only if necessary (ask for their fee structure up front), then put this part of the job search process in the Completed Column within the first week of your search.

A note about cover letters. As with the advice for resumes, be straightforward, professional and don't embellish. Address a specific role you are pursuing in the letter if you have this information and detail why you are a fit. It is also a good idea to share any personal connection or shared interest/history you might have with the person receiving your letter/resume.

There is one more thing to consider. Be cautious about soliciting several opinions from friends and recruiters about your resume. You will likely get a different opinion from each of them, which will only lead to more anxiety making you question your choices and slow you down. Pick one or two candid professionals in your network with resume reviewing experience to share their feedback.

Questions for Reflection:

1. Based on what I've read in this chapter, have I spent too much time, energy and money on my resume? Am I seeing results from my investment?
2. Can I make improvements like the ones suggested here? Is my resume too wordy and lacking in measurable results?
3. How has this chapter changed my perception of the role resumes play in the search process? Do I agree or disagree?

4. How many opinions have I sought out about my resume and how many times have I made changes based on this feedback?

Action Item:

Take the resume you currently possess and review it carefully using the lessons shared in this chapter. Make notes and highlight changes. Commit to having your revised resume completed within a few days of completing this book.

10 ADVANCED INTERVIEWING

Unlike my advice to not overthink resumes, I strongly encourage you to take interviewing seriously and over-prepare if possible. You have worked hard, followed the suggestions in each chapter of the book and are getting invited to interviews. This is great, but don't put your feet up just yet! You made it through the various minefields to earn an <u>opportunity</u> to interview, but the competition is fierce and you must stay focused.

Over the years, I have enjoyed not only interviewing candidates for my companies or clients, but I have also been insatiably curious about what candidates are doing and seeing in their job searches, especially with regards to interviews. The information I have been gathering has helped me develop a list of Best Practices for interviewing:

- *Do your homework.* Carefully research the company and the hiring manager(s) on the Internet. LinkedIn and Google are excellent resources for obtaining background information. Also, have questions ready for the person interviewing you. Never go to an interview unprepared.

- *Be nice to the receptionist.* This person is the company's emissary to the world and is quick to size people up. Be courteous, professional and friendly – much can be learned from a warm conversation. When I'm hiring, I always ask our receptionist for her experiences and impressions of the initial interaction. Most hiring managers I know do the same.

- *Have the basics down.* Dress professionally, bring copies of your resume on quality paper, turn off your smart phone (completely, don't let the vibrating text messages be a distraction), don't wear cologne or perfume, don't chew gum, arrive 15 minutes early, give quantifiable answers to questions, do not ramble and follow up with a thank-you note by dropping it off the next day if possible. It's surprising how many people don't get this right!

- *Make a personal connection.* You are looking to win an advocate for your candidacy as well as eventually get the job. Every person you meet in the interview process should tell the others involved, "He/she is a great candidate and good culture fit. I really like him/her." Remember that asking questions, commenting on pictures and diplomas in the office and highlighting shared interests changes an interview from hiring authority and candidate into two people having a friendly conversation.

- *Ask questions about culture in the interview.* What are the values and vision of the company? Research will tell you much of this, but hearing the answers directly from an employer will be more revealing and allow for a more exploratory dialogue. Make sure you share how you would fit the culture. Many candidates forget to do this.

- *Be clear and concise about why you are right for the job.* If you have done your homework, you will be able to relate specific parts of your background to the open position, emphasizing why you are the ideal candidate they seek. Also, do not forget to express your interest in the job. I frequently hear from clients about their concern that a candidate didn't seem excited enough or genuinely interested in the position. On the flip side, excitement is good, but be careful to not appear desperate.

- *Offer references in the interview.* Telling a hiring manager you strongly suggest they speak to someone who can describe your leadership of the sales team, for example, will make you look more credible.

- *Stay calm.* Nervousness leads to over-talking, which will negatively affect your chances of landing the position.

- *Remember, you are also there to interview the company* if you wish to make a sound choice. Don't finish the interview process without having your questions and concerns addressed or you may wind up looking for a new job again in six months.

In conjunction with the Interviewing Best Practices, I have also developed a short list of questions you should <u>never</u> ask in a first interview:

- *What is the compensation package like for this position?* There is a time and place for this question, and it is certainly not in the first interview. If you don't already know the salary range and bonus structure, it will be more comfortable to inquire about this in a later round of interviewing or possibly in a follow up call with human resources.

- *What is the career path for this position?* Again, not a first round interview question to ask. It looks like you are more interested in the next role instead of the one if front of you.

- *Do you offer flexible schedules?* Despite the expanding acceptance of flexible work schedules, asking this too early in the process makes you look like someone more concerned about your schedule than doing a great job for the company.

- *Who are your competitors?* This question and any like it reveal that you did not do your homework on the company. Everything is available online and basic company information should be known before the interview.

- *Why is the position open?* Not a bad question, but the interviewer may have shared that information with you 15 minutes ago. Be careful to not ask questions that make it appear you are not listening to the interviewer.

I sought out additional input on the subject of interviewing from professionals who have excellent experience on the subject. One such professional is Dr. Patty Kubus, whom I interviewed for another topic in Chapter Three. She focuses her skills and experience on executive coaching, executive selection and succession management.

Patty, what are the best ways for job seekers to prepare for the questions they will receive in job interviews?

"Job seekers must know themselves well – their motivators, learning style, strengths, development areas and experiences and accomplishments. Most interviewers do a fairly poor job of interviewing, which explains why there are so many selection failures. However, a skillful interviewer will ask the candidates the same questions (called a structured interview) so that they can evaluate all candidates on the same data set.

"They will also use what we call a behavioral method of interviewing, which is based on the premise that past behavior predicts future behavior. In a behavioral interview, the interviewer will have a list of competencies that are required for success in the particular job. They will then prepare questions for each of those competencies to help them discover how the candidate has performed previously on each of those competencies.

"For example, Decision Making is a skill required in most roles. The interviewer will design questions to help evaluate how you've actually made decisions in the past. They will be looking for a *specific* example of your decision making process. You might get a question like this:

'Tell me about an important decision you've made in your job. How did you go about this process? What was the result?'

"They will be looking for a specific example here, not how you would typically address this process. You should be prepared with 1-2 good examples to talk through, including a little bit about the situation, how you gathered data, analyzed it, generated alternatives, weighed them, selected the best option, implemented an action and evaluated the results.

"So, to prepare for an interview, think about the list of competencies you feel would be necessary for success in that particular role. Here is a list of four typical skills 'buckets' with some examples listed for each:

- *Interpersonal.* Some examples are: communication, building relationships, customer focus, managing conflict
- *Personal characteristics.* Some examples are: motivators, openness to change, results orientation, learning style
- *Management.* Some examples are: business and financial acumen, strategic planning, decision making, executing the plan, organization
- *Leadership.* Some examples are: delegating, coaching, mentoring talent, influencing, leading change, building teams, driving innovation

"You may not come up with the exact list that the interviewer has, but you will probably be quite close. Have a copy of your resume in front of you as you think back to determine the best examples to share. The best examples will be *recent, job-related* and *important occurrences.*

"You may also be asked about when things didn't work out as you had planned, perhaps a decision that did not yield optimal results. We all make mistakes. The interviewer wants to see if you recognize and own mistakes and learn from them. So, be honest.

"Having specific examples top of mind will help you give the interviewer the information they need. It will also help you stay relaxed an engaged. Trying to think of examples 'on the spot' will likely make you feel more stressed and diminish your personal impact. So, be prepared."

Are there any examples of questions you have encountered which typically cause challenges for candidates during interviews? How can they overcome those challenges?

"The behavioral examples discussed in the first question can trip people up because they don't prepare. Another area that can be challenging is organizational culture. That can be a nebulous concept for most people (candidates and interviewers alike) so it tends to be dismissed. But actually, culture misfit is the number one reason for candidate selection failure and should be considered to be of paramount importance.

"If an interviewer asks you to describe the type of organizational culture in which you excel, be ready to share your thoughts. Think about your values and motivators and determine where they fall in these areas:

- Support/Affiliation
- Achievement/Development
- Competition/Power

"Think about cultures where you have thrived and cultures where you struggled. How would you describe them? What was different about them? Why did you thrive in one culture and not the other? Being prepared will help to ensure that you are a good fit for the role and for the culture. If an interviewer never mentions organizational culture, be sure to ask them."

Seeking an additional knowledgeable resource on interviewing, I spoke with consultant, coach and former human resources leader, Lori Dubuc. Lori is the managing partner of Infinite Strategies Group, LLC and she has more than 20 years of human resources experience with both Fortune 500 and start-up companies, including leadership positions in human resources across a variety of industries. She is also a certified executive coach with the International Coach Federation.

Lori, please share your thoughts on some of the questions candidates should be asking themselves prior to beginning their next career search, which will help them be better prepared for interviews.

"Your first task is to take an inventory. Look at your life as an observer. What is it that you want to do, and what is it that would help draw the perfect picture of how you would like to see your life played out? Here are some specific questions to determine what you want next in a way that is purposeful. When reading these ideas, make them your own, and most importantly, answer them honestly in order for your next position be the right fit.

1. *What am I great at?* Each of us has a skill set that is our own. Some skills we love to use and others, not so much. This is an opportunity to think outside of the typical box of what you've done to determine where you excel. Think about past projects where you've lost track of time and truly enjoyed your work. With today's demand for talent, it may be an opportunity to reframe your idea of what you want into something that could provide you and an employer a great opportunity for growth.

2. *What are your priorities?* Are you striving for work/life balance and what does that look like for you? What are your budgetary needs and desires? If you are honest with yourself, why do you think you want to continue growing your career and what would be your ideal end game? When asking these questions as a coach, it's fascinating to see clients dig into their priorities and uncover what's meaningful or meaningless, and determine how their priorities shift their needs for that next role.

3. *What is the company culture that will provide you with the opportunity you need?* Is it a family-friendly atmosphere or a place where you get your work done and leave? Do they mentor their employees? What are their values?

4. *And specifically for those executives near or at retirement, what do you really want to do?* How do you envision 'work' in the next chapter of your life? Design it and you'll be surprised to find that companies will sometimes flex to what you design (within reason) and sometimes fit exactly what you're looking for. The talent shortage has really opened this market up to retirees. It's time to take an inventory again."

Are there other benefits you see to this process?

"Absolutely. Knowing what you want and don't want will help narrow down your response during networking and interviewing as to what you see as your ideal next role and company. When speaking with a recruiter or hiring manager, you want to be clear what that next position ideally looks like for you. One friend that is in the middle of a job search was able to narrow her field to human resources within a medium or large company where she has a direct impact on human capital. Her background was in large companies, and once she took an inventory of her 25+

year career, she became most excited when she was able to see the fruits of her labor. This has helped her to articulate to recruiters where she will compromise and more importantly, where she excels."

Based on the information in this chapter, you should be well equipped for your next interview. Remember: The underlying theme to all of this advice is to *be prepared*. Don't leave to chance one of the most critical stages of your job search.

Questions for Reflection:

1. How have my views on interviewing changed after reading this chapter? What will I do differently?
2. Following the advice of Dr. Kubus, am I prepared to share specific examples of my work, how I make decisions, etc.?
3. Lori Dubuc advocates taking an inventory of my skills before I begin interviewing. What does my personal inventory reveal? How will I be better prepared for future interviews with this knowledge?
4. Do I align with the author's Interviewing Best Practices and Questions to Avoid during the first interview? Can I see how not following these guidelines has derailed me in the past?

Action Item:

Follow Lori Dubuc's advice and write down a personal inventory of your skills and interests. Also, consider an unsuccessful interview from your past (when you did not win the job). Break down the interview and compare your performance with the knowledge you have gained in this chapter. Consider how you would perform if you had a chance at a do-over.

11 NEGOTIATING 101

The interviews have gone well and you have a realistic shot at landing a new job. You are in the last portion of your search journey, and in many ways this is the most crucial aspect of the process. Many job seekers I encounter are so consumed by finding a new job that they often forget to carefully consider their response when finally offered a new position. Negotiating an offer can produce a great deal of anxiety, especially if someone has been out of work for an extended period of time.

There is a successful approach I have seen candidates take in a negotiation process. The outcome may not always be a dramatic increase from the original offer, but generally candidates are able to win meaningful concessions from their future employer leaving both sides of the table feeling satisfied.

Here is a list of these Best Negotiating Practices:

- *Manage your emotions.* Stay calm, be patient, be professional, don't overreact and don't assume the worst during this process.
- *Share past compensation information.* You will always be asked, usually early in the process, what you are earning. Share your past compensation openly and candidly. This will be on the application anyway, so be honest.

- *"What sort of compensation package are you seeking?"* Don't be thrown off by this question. Answer it this way: "I am very interested in this opportunity and have thoroughly enjoyed our conversation. I would like to move forward in the process and learn more about your organization and the team. I will commit to you that I am open to a fair and compelling offer." If pushed further, perhaps say, "You know what I was earning before. I am open to the way the total package is structured, but certainly would prefer to avoid taking a step backward." It can be uncomfortable for many, but remember this: when you give a firm number, you are tied to that number. You may be underselling or eliminating yourself from further consideration by sharing specific numbers. If in the end you are forced to provide a specific number, share your research (you should already have this completed) on what the market is for your role and use the midpoint of the range as a guide.

- *Address benefits early.* An HR representative or the company web site will likely be the source of this information. Do not bring this up in your first meeting with a hiring manager, but try to determine if the healthcare and vacation coverage are adequate for your needs. Also, remember benefits can be part of the bargaining process as well. Rising healthcare costs completely justify added scrutiny in this area.

- *Always get an offer in writing.* Verbal offers are acceptable, but must be followed by a written offer. There is often a strong desire from some employers to have an immediate answer, but you should always ask for some time to consider the offer – taking a few days is absolutely acceptable. Evaluate it very carefully and consider the overall offer, your negotiable points and where you will not be able to budge.

- *If you think there is an opportunity to negotiate, explore the subject carefully and professionally with the decision maker.* For example, "I am very excited about the offer and look forward to a great career with your company. We are very close on the terms, but wonder if you could consider increasing the base in order to keep me whole from my last position and also add a week of vacation, again to match what I had before. Your health benefits kick in after 90 days, which means I will be on COBRA during that time. Can you pick up that cost or help me offset it in some way? Everything else looks fantastic and I am hoping we can come to terms soon on these other points as I am eager to start."

- *Be creative.* Sometimes the main issue for the company is keeping the offer within their budget, yet they may have flexibility with how the money is spent. For example, the offer may contain a substantial relocation package that exceeds your needs. Consider asking for a portion of the relocation budget as a sign-on bonus instead.

- *Protect yourself.* The company will usually offer a package that protects them and mitigates their risk. For example, the offer may appear generous with everything in line, but much of the compensation is attached to the performance bonus. If this is a new role or if the position has a history of challenges, consider asking for a portion of the bonus to be guaranteed. The reasoning is this will give you time to get up to speed and protect your earnings during this ramp-up period.

- *You will likely only have a maximum of two exchanges in the negotiating process.* Hiring managers may begin to lose patience with you if the process is not brought to a successful conclusion on the second exchange, so choose your words and requests carefully and ask for everything you want in the first pass.

- *Trust and transparency are key.* If you have a trusting relationship with a recruiter and are open about your needs, this can make the negotiating process go smoothly. You also have an opportunity, through the recruiter, to communicate exactly what you are seeking to the company. I prefer to have a candidate tell me their bottom line so I can guide my client to make their most compelling offer up front, thus eliminating the need for further negotiation.

- *When handling multiple offers, timing is everything.* Don't allow any of the companies making offers to feel like you are stringing them along or playing them against each other. If you keep asking for more time so you can get an additional offer, this could backfire. Make up your mind as quickly as you can and make the choice. Delaying this decision can lead to ill feeling and even a retraction of the offer.

- *Go to your trusted advisors.* Be willing to discuss the negotiations with a few trusted and candid advisors. Listen to them as they might see something you missed.

What about other perspectives? I had the good fortune to interview someone for this chapter who has experienced negotiating as both a candidate and hiring manager. Virginia Means is a former consultant, business owner and senior human resources leader who is currently a Director of Human Resources for one of the nation's leading healthcare organizations.

Virginia, given your experience, you are likely no stranger to the art of negotiation. What would be your advice for a candidate negotiating a job offer?

"Remember that timing is everything – unless the employer mentions money, don't discuss it until after you receive an offer. Remember that negotiations are not typically processed at the same speed as a Google search. Offers involve people and they take time. Be patient and respectful during the process.

"A number of factors can be negotiated in an offer so know what's most important to you, such as learning new skills, flexibility, vacation time, educational sponsorship, reimbursement of certain clubs/professional memberships, cash compensation, etc. Do your homework to understand what your skills are worth in the marketplace – don't go into an interview process without understanding what a reasonable salary is in the current market. Keep in mind that salaries fluctuate just like other marketplace factors."

Have you developed best or worst practices lists for negotiation? Would you mind sharing?

"I have because there are so many critical elements to the process. I'll share them here.

Best Practices for Negotiation

- *Avoid premature negotiation.* Before you try to negotiate anything, be sure that the company is interested in hiring you. If you attempt to bargain too early in the interview process, it can be perceived as a negative, which can take you from the lead candidate to the bottom of the list.

- *Preface any negotiation with a positive.* Start talking money only after you've thanked the employer for the offer and let them know how much you look forward to adding value to the organization.
- *Leave the personal stuff out of your negotiation.* Only discuss concrete ways in which you will contribute to the company's profits, and are therefore worth a salary increase.
- *When the time is right, share your research with the prospective employer.* Citing tables, charts, facts and figures from respected sources shows the interviewer that you have done your homework and know what you're talking about. (See Appendix 4 for useful resources on this subject.)
- *Be professional.* Even if the initial offer is low, maintain grace and an upbeat dialog with the company.
- *Know your bottom line.** Based on your research, determine the least amount you can and are willing to take. If you are genuinely interested in the job, but a gap remains in cash compensation, during the negotiation phase ask for a salary review in three or six months. If they agree, this will give you some time to demonstrate your contribution to the organization and make way for some flexibility in your pay."

Worst Practices for Negotiation

- *Jump the gun.* Don't launch into the money discussion before the employer brings it up.
- *Make it all about you.* Employers don't want to hear that you can't make your car payment unless they increase your salary offer.
- *Be afraid to negotiate.* After the initial offer, most organizations expect that candidates will take a swing at ratcheting up the initial deal.
- *Request an unreasonable package.* If the number is exorbitant when you ask for a salary, negotiations may stop – cold."

What was the toughest negotiation you've handled over your career? Why does this one stand out in your memory?

"I had never been in a C-suite role before, but was extended an offer and had no idea what the newly created position was worth in the marketplace. The CEO asked what it would take, and didn't know how to respond. So, I told him I needed to think about it and would reach back out the following day. I quickly called several of my mentors and received some excellent advice from one of them: 'Ask for a compensation package similar to the other suits around the boardroom table.' So, I did. This was my favorite advice because it allowed for some flexibility, rather than giving an exact number, and put the ball in his court. The next day, he came to me with a package above my expectations, which is probably why this one stands out in my memory."

Entire books have been written about negotiation, but I hope these insights will help you prepare when faced with this exciting dilemma. I stress again to be calm and patient despite feeling eager to say "yes" and get started. A poorly negotiated offer could lead to frustrations later on, even causing you to leaving this great new job. Preparation can prevent all that.

Questions for Reflection:

1. After reading this chapter, which of the Best Practices provided do I feel I am prepared to do now? Which ones do I need to work on developing?
2. Have I taken a personal inventory and do I know what I really want from a job offer? Can I articulate what I really want to others?
3. Am I comfortable with the concept of negotiating? If not, who in my circle can I trust to help me through this piece of the process?
4. Can I recall a time when I negotiated poorly before taking a new role? What has this chapter taught me about handling that particular situation if faced with it again?

Action Item:

In your job search journal, write down your non-negotiable items for a future offer. Also, write down your realistic compensation expectations (backed up by research) and break it down by salary, bonus potential and benefits as well as other factors potentially important to you, such as car allowance, flexibility, education reimbursement, etc.

SECTION IV

OTHER THINGS TO CONSIDER

12 TURNING AGE INTO AN ASSET

It is a common tale these days – a 60-something senior leader in career transition has a series of job interviews since departing his last role, but nothing to show for it. Another leader with a long track record of success in her 30-year career struggles to even get interviews. Another candidate in his 50's realizes after he is downsized that he doesn't know enough people who can help him in his job search.

They all wonder what they are doing wrong. "Is it my resume?" "Have I forgotten how to interview?" "How do I build a network from scratch?" "Do I need to hire a career coach?" "Why don't companies realize my value?" "Am I still relevant?" They may also wonder if they are a casualty of age bias.

As I've interviewed candidates in career transition over the years, I've drawn specific conclusions about helping professionals like the ones mentioned here. This chapter is meant to be helpful to three distinct groups:

1. Employers who have open positions for which these professionals may be a fit.

2. Professionals over the age of 45 in career transition.

3. Anyone else who will join the preceding groups at some point in his or her career.

Reconsidering Seasoned Workers in Today's Workforce – Advice for Companies

I choose to believe companies have the best intentions with regards to hiring seasoned employees. I think the real challenge for them is a need to embrace more creative approaches to staffing and develop internal training to best utilize the skills and talents of more experienced professionals. Part of the problem comes in when we apply these assumptions:

- *"Older employees don't work well when supervised by younger employees."* Instead of assuming this is the case, purposely pair a younger employee in need of training and development with someone more experienced and see the end result. This mentoring relationship can pay big dividends to all involved (especially the Millennials) if handled and managed appropriately.

- *"If they accept a position with a lesser title and reduced income they will leave as soon as they can find a more suitable job."* Trust someone if they say they won't leave for a better opportunity. Consider offering a sign-on bonus that has to be paid back if the employee leaves within a year or two. With many companies looking carefully at their (often low) employee engagement scores, investing in our employees and making them feel appreciated is often the best way to avoid turnover.

- *"They don't fit our exact position requirements so there is nothing we can do."* I consistently question why companies don't more proactively add talent to their mix as consultants or contractors. It is a great way to bring their experience and expertise into the organization. A little creative scheduling and training for internal hiring managers could help companies tap into a vast pool of talent in a cost-effective way.

- *"Older employees are too set in their ways and not coachable. We can also hire who we need for a lot less money."* Older employees are often more coachable than the emerging Gen Y population. Hiring someone with less experience and lower income requirements because you think they are more coachable may in fact be setting that individual up to fail. Typically, older employees possess not only strong experience, but maturity and perspective as well. They may be more expensive, or may not. They do offer unique professional qualities and may even be at a place in their lives where income is no longer their primary motivation.

There are several approaches an organization might take in tackling this growing issue and I hope we will see more open-mindedness and creativity from Corporate America when considering older employees in the future.

Taking Stock – Advice for Candidates

You have been through countless work experiences and dealt with a host of unique situations. You have worked through good and bad economic cycles. And, you have likely accumulated your own "best practices" in dealing with a host of people and business issues. Write these down alongside a list of skills and things you are passionate about at this point in your career. Now, what do you do with this information?

Your experience to date is your greatest asset as you consider a new or better job. Are you using it appropriately? Being aware of your gifts, skills and passions is only the start. The challenge is to use this information to focus on the career opportunities that allow you to add the most value to a prospective employer. Describe your assets in a compelling and succinct summary – this is vitally important, but often overlooked. Reflect on the possible causes of any reluctance to hire you and consider these five actionable ideas:

1. *Do your homework.* Utilize the Wall Street Journal, your local business journal, Google, LinkedIn, ZoomInfo and old-fashioned networking to understand what "pain point" a company is facing. This research will enable you to tailor (not embellish) your experiences and successes in a compelling way that will make you more attractive to a prospective employer if they are facing problems you have dealt with previously.

2. *Offer to mentor the next generation.* Half of the U.S. workforce will exit in the next 15 years as the Baby Boomers and older Gen Xers retire. This means Gen Y will rise at an ever-increasing rate into leadership roles. Are they prepared? The majority of business leaders would say no. Your experience can be a tremendous asset to an organization concerned about developing this younger generation. Present yourself as a mentor and coach who will help prepare them to lead.

3. *Alter expectations.* In this shifting economy, it may be difficult to maintain a comparable title and salary while looking for a new opportunity. Are you at a place in life where a smaller title and less income are possible? This is a difficult consideration, but weigh this decision against being unemployed for a year while holding out for the "right" job. It is smart to consider this possibility early in the job search, rather than later. You can always supplement your income by doing something else you love.

4. *Work for yourself.* Why not start your own business or become a consultant for hire? Create a basic LLC or divide your time among a few companies as a contractor to help them tackle important projects. Candidates rarely think to suggest this in an interview, but with healthcare costs skyrocketing and employee headcount a concern, more companies are turning to consultants and part-time employees. Don't expect the employer to offer the option to be a contractor, you will need to bring it up. They may be looking for a long-term fit for the role, but you might be the perfect person to temporarily bridge the gap.

5. *Remain relevant and fight stereotypes.* There has long been an assumption that people over a certain age are not social media savvy and don't know how to network. In my experience, becoming proficient at LinkedIn, Facebook and Twitter is not difficult, nor age specific. The key is recognizing that you want to build an attractive personal brand and these tools can help you do that and get your message out to the right people. LinkedIn is especially helpful in the business community.

Some Brief Do's and Don'ts

As you embark on this journey of finding a new role at this stage of your life, there are some basic do's and don'ts that are important to remember:

- *Do* pay it forward and offer to help others as you are seeking help.
- *Do* your homework. Talk to as many people as possible who have been down the path you want to travel. Learn all you can and use this knowledge to develop a creative approach to your search.
- *Do* the math. You need to talk a lot of people in your search. Set goals for reaching out to at least 10 people a day and plan coffee/lunch with a viable networking contact on a daily basis.
- *Do* remain upbeat and positive. Exude confidence and believe in your value.
- *Don't* burn out your network. Be respectful of their time and ask for help in a way that is easy for them. They want to help, but you may not be the most important thing on their to-do list. For tips on utilizing your network effectively, see Chapter Four, The Unconnected Leader.
- *Don't* wait for your next job to fall in your lap. You have to be highly visible within your markets, as uncomfortable as it may be for some, meeting new people and uncovering opportunities that make sense for you.
- *Don't* be bitter, give up or blame others. This victim mentality is never helpful. It turns off the very people who might be able to help you. Channel the negative energy you are wasting into trying new approaches to your search.
- *Don't* be inflexible. Keep an open mind and be creative when discussing a new role and compensation.

This subject is vast, but my sincere hope is the few insights shared here will provide more seasoned job seekers with encouragement, direction and perhaps a few new ideas. Job seekers of any age can often experience a loss of self-esteem and self-confidence, which can be debilitating. I encourage employers to tap into this experienced and valuable group of professionals in creative ways to harness the positive contributions they are eager to make.

Questions for Reflection:

1. After reading this chapter, did I learn the various ways to turn age into an asset? Do these suggestions resonate with me?
2. If necessary, can I consider (now or in the future) becoming a consultant instead of only working in a full-time role?
3. Have I ever been guilty of making the assumptions outlined in the first section of the chapter? Can I change? Have I ever been on the receiving end of these assumptions? Can I facilitate change?
4. I understand from this chapter that I must be able to package and sell my skills, regardless of my age. Am I prepared to do this?

Action Item:

Approach #1 – If you are over 45 and feeling frustrated about your job search, make a list of the changes you need to make and refer back to the elements in the chapter frequently to make sure you are seeing improvement.

Approach #2 – If you are under 45 and do not consider your age to be an issue (yet), consider making a plan now for how to avoid these challenges in the future. Consider the skills you will need to acquire if you choose to pursue consulting in the future.

13 SHOULD I GO INTO BUSINESS FOR MYSELF?

Can you envision working for yourself? Has the thought ever occurred to you? As mentioned in the last chapter, starting your own business is a viable option that should be carefully considered. Here are a few reasons why:

- The economic outlook and potential implications of the Affordable Care Act project significant advantages for part-time workers and consultants in the near future as employers look to reduce healthcare expenses for full-time employees.
- There may be opportunities to contract or consult with previous employers as companies look to bring more of that type of workforce into their talent mix. Companies may have lay-offs, but still need the skills and expertise of their people.
- Taking on consulting or project work during a career transition period provides income and will eliminate a significant employment gap on the resume.
- As countless professionals have done, consulting is a great fit for many in the later stage of life, and you may decide to make the shift a permanent one.

There are a few challenges to consider before making this move:

- If health benefits are not available from another source, or if the cost of providing your own benefits is cost prohibitive, this option may not be workable.

- Be certain you have skills that are in demand – and you know how to market them appropriately to the right audience. Ensure you conduct research on a fair rate for your services in order to avoid selling yourself short.

- If your goal is still full-time employment, don't overcommit to consulting work that doesn't allow you to run an active job search.

- Consult with an accountant to understand the tax implications of working for yourself.

You may be thinking, "Can I really do this?" The hesitation is understandable. In order to gain helpful insights into this type of transition, I sought out the opinions of two professionals who have successfully made the leap and one who is weighing his options carefully before making this choice.

My first interview is with Dr. Kym Harris, a former human resources executive who is now CEO of Your SweetSpot Coaching and Consulting, LLC. Dr. Harris works with diverse professionals, leaders and executives to maximize their professional and personal potential. She also guides organizations in maximizing the potential of their human capital through executive coaching, leadership development and group coaching for employee resource groups.

Kym, having gone from an HR leader to a successful consulting career with a brief period of unemployment in between, can you share with job seekers how you made the transition?

"I always wanted to ensure I had options if my employment situation changed. For me that meant leveraging education to expand my skills and add to my credentials. As a result, I was able to transfer the strengths and talents I developed throughout my 20+ year career into executive coaching and consulting. I have taken the aspects of my career I enjoyed the most and made them my focus.

"During my transitional period, I actually pursued employment opportunities *and* began to lay the foundation for my coaching and consulting business. The more I worked on the business, the more attractive doing my own thing became. I'm intentional about nurturing my existing relationships and cultivating new ones, which has helped a great deal. I also sought out coaches and mentors to advise and educate me further because entrepreneurship is new to me. I think the largest obstacle for individuals making this type of transition is finances. I had to overcome my fear of financial instability and have faith that if I was committed to and purposeful in my work, my financial needs would be met. There is also a mental hurdle to overcome and having the self-confidence to lean into your talents. Every day, I just kept moving forward and with each success, my confidence grew."

Is consulting for everyone? Are there things you wish you had done differently as you established your business?

"No, consulting is not for everyone. There is a discipline that must be maintained to keep the pipeline filled with prospects, ensure timely follow-up and complete the administrative tasks that I am used to asking someone else to do. Additionally, selling and the rejection that comes with that can be a challenge. I have learned to leverage my relationship building skills and have established a rhythm that does not feel like selling. I have also learned that every person and every organization is not my ideal client, so saying 'no' is no longer an issue for me.

"If I had to identify something I wish I had done differently, it would be related to a few of my financial expenditures. A viable business must have cash. I am learning that I can do more than I thought possible with little to no cash outlay. When larger expenditures are required, I have learned to take the time to do much more research before spending. Investing the time to do my homework has been a considerable cost savings."

Is consulting the only option when someone wishes to leave the corporate world? Are there other opportunities you may have considered?

"I considered teaching at the college/university level and actually tried it for a couple of semesters, but did not enjoy it as much as I thought I would. I still play with the idea of purchasing a franchise, but the financial investment requires that I wait before moving forward. Half of my career was spent on the administrative side of higher education, but while I enjoyed the environment, I left because of the salary.

"There are so many things out there to explore, and they don't have to be related to what you've been doing. One of my brothers established his own construction company after being downsized. His background was in insurance, but he liked the idea of building communities and beautifying neighborhoods. So, he sat for the licensing exams and now he runs a successful construction business. I think it is important for someone in transition to consider a few things when thinking of the possibilities: What skills do I have? Do I enjoy doing what my skills and experience have prepared me to do? What other careers/professions have I considered over the years? What would it take to move in that direction? What would I do if I knew I could not fail?"

Another professional who made the transition to consulting is Vicki Hamilton. Vicki is a senior IT/Operations executive consultant who develops new IT strategies to take care of old workplace problems. In addition, she has been internationally published, writing a monthly mentoring column for South Africa's *CEO Magazine*. Due to her passion for mentoring, she has launched a global online matchmaking mentoring program at www.thewrightanswer.net.

Vicki, when you left your senior leadership role with a Fortune 50 company, what was your focus in terms of finding a new job?

"Due to contractual obligations, I was not able to work and receive payments for about 14 months. So, I took this time to do some free consulting for organizations that needed technology strategy and operational assistance. This gave me a chance to really think about what I wanted to do next. During this time, I continued to keep my eyes open for the next opportunity. I knew that at my level, time was not my friend and it could take a while. I focused on networking, keeping my skills sharp and giving back.

"As I looked for the next opportunity, I considered other possibilities within my industry, functional expertise and comparable skill set requirements. As the days passed, I did receive notifications about jobs, but due to the job market at the time, companies could afford to be as particular as they wanted for each role. Whether they wanted internal company knowledge, exact industry experience, years of certain technology expertise – the bottom line is that it just wasn't happening.

"I began to think about starting my own thing. Just working for myself and with clients with whom I could help move forward. There were three primary aspects – project based work, professional services and CEO advisory services. As I looked at companies, I had the choice to pick the right culture, the right opportunity and have flexibility at the same time."

As you considered the various opportunities in the job market, I am curious about how you found these. Was it through recruiters? Networking?

"I used several techniques to find the right clients and right opportunities. One, I looked at job openings, since they are an immediate indication of 'holes within the organization.' I then looked at leaders within those companies and within my network to learn more about the real need of the organizations. I reached out to offer consulting services to the hiring manager focusing on one major thing that I could do to help fill the gap while they looked for the right person. For one client, the President was looking for a COO. She brought me on to do strategy for the company's technology and business goals, as well as be her personal technical advisor. Not only was this a great match, but also a win-win for everyone involved.

"I also partnered with other consultants to help fill in when executive talent was needed. I used all of my network connections and vendors, with whom I worked with in the past as a customer. I know they understood my capabilities and the quality that I would bring to the table. This allowed me to get involved with a much larger base of clients and continue to grow my consulting experience, which proved to be very viable. I am still leveraging these relationships and gaining long-term clients.

"Lastly, I keep my network updated on where I am with my clients. I begin to look for the next opportunities about four months out, so I can be ready when one engagement ends to start another. My network includes LinkedIn connections, organizations, recruiters, board members, family, friends, church members and other entrepreneurs."

How did you discern that starting your own consulting business was the right approach for your career?

"When you look for a next career move and things do not start to happen, you must take control of the situation. I have always had a strategy in mind, if I lost my job, I would go into consulting or teaching. I began teaching as an adjunct professor, putting that master's degree to work.

I have a very strong faith and asked God to show me the right thing to do. After I began consulting, I knew this was my destiny. Additionally, my personal life was changing with caring for aging parents, and an ill brother and brother-in-law. As these things began to happen, I needed flexibility in a different way. I needed to be able to work from anywhere, travel as needed and continue to make a living. Consulting gave me that opportunity and more. As of today, I have contracts that last for another year and doing what I am supposed to do. Although, I will always be open to look at the next fork in the road to determine the next direction."

What have been the most significant career and life lessons you've learned within the last few years?

"I have learned that although working for yourself has a lot of benefits, you definitely have to work and think differently. Here are some examples of what I'm talking about:

1. If you don't work, you don't get paid. Therefore, there is no such thing as going on vacation and getting a paycheck. You must plan for it.

2. Plan for your financial security from a retirement perspective. No one is contributing to your 401k, except you.
3. Taxes and expenses are in the forefront of your mind. You know that you must think about every move strategically as you alone bear the burden.
4. Flexibility can come at a cost, but it is worth it when you need it. Especially when trying to balance the more important things in life – your family and your ability to be there for them.
5. Nothing stays the same forever so count on change as part of the equation. Being in business today can shift to working for someone else tomorrow under the right circumstances. Be prepared and flexible to embrace these changes."

Finally, I was fortunate to spend time with business executive, Sam Robb, who had taken a severance package from his organization and was beginning the process of evaluating his options. Sam has more than 30 years of progressing sales and marketing leadership roles with Fortune 100 companies. He still has a great deal to offer and is excited about this next chapter of his life.

Sam, you have had a long and successful career in sales and marketing for large companies. What are you seeking for the next chapter in your career and why?

"I have been fortunate to work with some really fine organizations, wonderful bosses and have exceeded my wildest dreams in terms of achievement. But, I do believe big organizations need to reinvent themselves to promote and build fresh talent. This means there comes a time when 'you're in the way' of progress if you're a long-standing incumbent. That is the fork in the road I have encountered and it is neither good nor bad – it is just reality. It's time to move on and help smaller and mid-size outfits benefit from many years of productive and enriching experiences."

Consulting is not for the faint of heart, but it can be an excellent choice for people with great subject matter expertise and a strong network. How do you make the transition into consulting work financially and emotionally?

"I have just begun the process of designing what the brand and the product might look like, so I'm not 100 percent sure I can answer the question credibly. The way I'm thinking about it now is that you need to be sure you have a good handle on your economic and personal balance sheet. Economic – are you ready to assume risk? Personal – will people buy into your product? Economically, I am good (not perfect), and personally, I'm not 100 percent sure. When you work for a big company and have a big job, you tend to be fashionable and in demand. When left on your own without the company security blanket, you'll learn pretty quickly who cares."

As you consider the next move in your career, what resources will you draw on to help you make this decision?

"Great question. I continue to be overwhelmed with the role LinkedIn plays in today's job market. I have added close to a thousand contacts over many years, and I'm using it to reconnect with folks that may have an interest in my game – not to mention all the pre-call insights on people and companies."

As you consider starting your own business, or consulting or working part-time while you continue pursuing full-time employment, carefully weigh every option. Many potentially great entrepreneurs have failed due to a lack of prudent planning. On the other hand, being your own boss may just be the most energizing and lucrative step you ever make in your career.

Questions for Reflection:

1. Am I prepared to go out on my own? What have I learned about this decision and am I prepared to take this leap of faith in my career?
2. What special skills and experiences do I have and is there a market for what I offer?
3. Is there a way I can work part-time or on project work and still continue my job search? Who in my network might employ me part-time?
4. Does my situation resemble any of the stories in this chapter or is it unique? If so, who in my network can I speak with to

learn more and allow me to make a more informed decision?

Action Item:

Make an honest list of your skills, strengths and experiences. Then, carefully consider what needs in the marketplace are underserved and determine if you are qualified to fill them. This is an excellent exercise to go through before making the decision to strike out on your own. If in doubt, solicit the honest advice from your trusted advisors.

14 THE PROBLEM WITH (TOO MUCH) ENCOURAGEMENT

"You're the best!" "You are right on track." "You can do anything!" "Your resume is perfect." I really like encouragement, like most people. I like to receive it and share it with the people in my life. The positive aspects of encouragement are numerous, but do we ever consider for a moment that too much encouragement is a bad thing? One group struggling with the adverse effects of other's good intentions are those in career transition.

Having a sizable network and a reputation for helping professionals in need of advice, I am often referred these good people on a weekly basis. By the time I encounter them, they have usually been looking for a job at least a month (with some having been out of work for well over a year). I am frequently surprised when I discover that the candid advice I offer in our meeting – for getting back on track in their job search – is often the first time they have heard critical coaching on ways to improve or alter their strategy. When I probe as to why, I discover that their circle of friends is providing wonderful encouragement, but almost no critical and helpful feedback.

Again, encouragement is not a bad thing. But, too much encouragement plus the absence of candid advice can potentially cripple the job search efforts of the friends we care about and delay their finding employment. So, how do we help?

Let's consider common reasons why some only want to offer encouragement:

- They fear giving candid feedback will lower the other person's self-esteem or hurt their feelings.

- Political correctness has seeped into our culture to an extreme and people seem more reluctant to have authentic and meaningful conversations.

- They could be part of the generation of parents (or they may be children of these parents) who only want to offer praise and encouragement to their children.

When we insist that every child wins a trophy for simply being on the team, or we consistently tell kids they are amazing for often mediocre or average effort, we are setting them up for failure in the real world as they grow accustomed to unrealistic expectations. It might feel good, but it's not helpful. The same is true for our peers seeking honest feedback.

What are some of the negative outcomes of giving too much encouragement without candid feedback?

- The job seeker loses valuable time and even extends their ranks among the unemployed because they are not addressing their real issues. They simply never knew because no one told them.

- An overdose of encouragement leads to over inflated and unrealistic expectations not connected to reality.

- The job seeker is often subjected to bigger disappointments from the flawed job search strategy no one addressed, versus the short-term discomfort of hearing from a friend that changes are necessary.

The problem grows exponentially over time. As a job seeker gets to a certain period of the search, let's say six months or more, there is a definite fear of hurting their confidence and self-esteem and giving candid advice is avoided more than ever.

To obtain this critical and balanced feedback, here are four practical suggestions for the job seeker:

- Balance your circle of friends with people who will tell you the other side of the story, even if it isn't all wine and roses. These are the people who care enough about you to share what you might not want to hear, and they are to be highly valued.

- Seek feedback from people beyond your network of friends: former co-workers and bosses, recruiters, etc. and solicit their candid assessment of your approach to finding a new job. They will likely have no agenda and their feedback can be enormously beneficial.

- Give your friends (and others) permission to be candid. You will have to make it clear you are sincerely asking them to be brutally honest about your job search process, or else they will fear offending you.

- Be self-aware and humble. This may not be easy, but it is important to acknowledge that the issue may be you. Maybe you turn people off in interviews because you do all the talking. Maybe your resume doesn't adequately explain your career history. Maybe you have a poor elevator pitch. Whatever the issue, acknowledge that you can always improve.

As someone offering advice, what is to be gained by having our peers leave us with less than our honest opinion? Straight talk, given out of love, is one of the best gifts we can offer a person. I often ask permission to be candid before I share critical feedback. This is usually appreciated and works well for me.

If you are a job seeker, stop accepting meaningless platitudes and insist that your friends, advisors and family tell you what they really think. You will be grateful as you make the corrections necessary to find your next job and get back to work.

Seeking an experienced voice from the trenches, I reached out to Paige Barry for her insights. Paige is an IT executive in the financial technology industry who began teaching job search skills after her own five-month unemployment in 2006. I was specifically interested in Paige's views on encouragement because she has lived through making the most common job search mistakes, and as a result, teaches a class bimonthly to help others avoid the same pitfalls.

Paige, do you come across professionals in career transition being derailed by too much encouragement?

"I think it is human nature to surround ourselves with people who love and support us, especially during times of suffering and loss. Though we need people to lift us up and encourage us, individuals looking for work need candid and frequent feedback.

"I often meet job seekers who struggle with interviews, both over the phone and in-person. In only a couple of cases in my seven years as a volunteer job search coach have I found someone who demonstrated the initiative to improve their interview skills by asking a colleague for a mock interview. Mock interviews can be indispensable in two ways: 1) it is a 'safe' environment for learning what you do well and not as well when speaking about yourself and your professional accomplishments, and 2) it can be an excellent way to network with employed professionals.

"When I conduct mock interviews, I observe the job seekers non-verbal communication. I also observe whether their answers have an obvious beginning, middle and end. For job seekers who do especially well during a mock interview, I attempt to lead them into revealing more about themselves than they might intend by making them feel at ease and asking questions unrelated to their work experience. In every case, a mock interview has provided feedback that has enabled the job seeker to do things just a little differently."

In your opinion, how does too much encouragement affect a job seeker? What is the downside?

"Too much encouragement disables a job seeker by allowing them to execute their job search with blinders on. I see this manifest in two ways. First, too many job seekers wait to seek guidance on how to effectively search for a job until after they have failed to achieve acceptable results. I experienced this myself. I spent a minimum of 30 hours a week looking for work for three months without getting a single job interview before I began asking 'why' from other professionals who had been in transition and had already successfully Landed.

"Second, too few job seekers employ the use of weekly goals and status reporting to track their efforts. When I meet frustrated job seekers, one of my first questions to them is, 'How many jobs have you applied to in the last 2-3 weeks?' Few know the exact number. If I ask them to show me where they are tracking their job search information, I often see spiral notebooks containing daily notes that are not organized in a way that facilitates quick retrieval of information."

What advice can you offer job seekers to overcome this problem?

"I often compare effective job search strategies to effective weight-loss strategies. If I set a goal to lose 'some' weight before next summer, my goal is vague and hard to track. If I set a goal to lose 20 pounds by Memorial Day, I can break my goal down into weekly increments and then measure myself against that goal every week. Looking for a job requires the same specificity.

"Job seekers need a plan for how many resumes, emails, phone calls and networking meetings they accomplish each week of their search. Since looking for a job is a full time endeavor for the unemployed, it is appropriate to write up a weekly status report that measures one's results against one's plan. This status report can be shared with a fellow job seeker or a former colleague. The key is for the job seeker to select someone who is willing to scrutinize each status report and provide guidance to the job seeker on how better results might be obtained. Do not pick someone who always compliments you and says encouraging things.

"This strategy is a way of creating a boss for ourselves while we look for a job. It can be very motivating to the job seekers knowing that they have to report their output on a weekly basis, as well as knowing someone is expecting their status report once a week."

Ultimately, you alone are responsible for the success of your job search. But, having accountability partners and candid friends can help you stay on track. Support should be welcomed and encouragement is wonderful, but begin valuing the opinions of those who don't always say what you want to hear.

Questions for Reflection:

1. Do I receive too much general encouragement and little candid feedback? Do I strongly encourage others to tell me what they really think and portray an open mind to constructive comments?
2. Can I reflect on times when my blindsides have caused me to not get an interview or a job offer? Would the advice of a candid friend have helped me be better prepared?
3. Have I tried the idea of a job accountability partner? Who do I know who will hold me accountable?
4. Is it difficult to admit that the problem with my search could be me? Do I struggle with self-awareness? Wouldn't the discomfort of candid feedback be better than being blindsided by mistakes I am making?

Action Item:

In your job search journal, write down a list of things that may be slowing or derailing your job search. Be honest with yourself. Reach out to the most candid people you know and ask for their input on the list as well. Develop a plan to overcome each obstacle as you move forward. And keep those friends close to you.

15 HOW DO I WORK WITH COMPANY RECRUITERS & SEARCH FIRMS?

At some point in your job search, you will interact with hiring managers, internal recruiters and possibly executive search firms. How you interact with them can have an enormous impact, positive or negative, on your success in landing a new job. Also, understanding the functions and goals of these professionals can make your job search go more smoothly and reduce overall anxiety. Here are some honest observations based on my experience:

Hiring Managers are the most important target for the job seeker. This person is hopefully your future boss and likely the key decision maker in the interview process. Beyond doing well in the interview, it is important that you build a personal connection with this person. Do your homework through LinkedIn, Google or discreetly through your contacts to learn more about him or her. Identify what you might have in common during the appropriate time in the interview. Having the hiring manager view you as a fellow parent, alumni from the same school or as a person who shares an interest in their favorite causes gives you a distinct advantage over other candidates who ignore this approach.

Caution! First and foremost, make the convincing argument you are the right professional for the job. Making a personal connection is an important, but *secondary consideration*. Also, do not forget to express interest in the role if you genuinely have one. Closing the hiring manager on why you should be selected is also an important part of the process.

Helpful Tip: If you know someone who is connected to the hiring manager and knows both of you well, ask your contact to make a proactive call on your behalf to the hiring manager before your interview. This strengthens your candidacy.

Internal Recruiters play an important and often overlooked role in the process. An internal recruiter proactively looking for candidates may have contacted you, or he or she may have contacted you upon the submission of your resume and application for a specific role. The internal recruiters I have encountered are generally overworked and extremely busy. They will not likely try to build a relationship with you as their main goal is to qualify you as a viable candidate and move you through the process. Your best approach is to be alert and focused when answering their questions as they are likely looking for certain responses. If they are open to answering your questions, try to learn as much as possible about the role, why it is open, the hiring manager's personality, etc. in order to answer the interview questions more intelligently and thoroughly.

Caution! Do not look past the internal recruiter. You must respect their role in the interview process. Generally, if they do not recommend you, the process will end there.

Helpful Tip: Study the job description carefully before speaking with an internal recruiter to make sure you can offer credible answers to their questions about how you fit the role.

Executive Search Firms do not necessarily have a great reputation for taking good care of candidates. The biggest criticism is often around communication and lack of follow up. This may or not be deserved, but realize that a search firm works for their client company who has hired them to find the right candidate for their open position. My firm interviews 3,000+ candidates a year and typically places 100-150 candidates, so we meet an enormous number of professionals who we do not place into an open position. Search firms can be a huge asset to you as they often have strong relationships with companies that may interest you.

Caution! Ask about a search firm's reputation through your network. Check out the employees of the firm and see how long they have worked there. Many new employees could be a sign of high turnover and other problems. This exploration may help you avoid working with firms that might not be helpful or even hinder your progress.

Helpful Tip: Although you should respect the role of the search firm and the people you interact with in their organization, you should expect the same respect as well. Ask for candid feedback and straightforward communications and offer the same.

While writing this book, I had meetings with two senior HR executives at large companies, as well as a former candidate who recently Landed a senior leadership role with a Fortune 50 company. I interviewed them on the subject of how candidates should work with hiring managers and internal recruiters.

The first interview is with Greg Jackson, Vice President of Talent Acquisition and Planning for a national multi-billion dollar technology and media company. Greg oversees a top-notch recruiting group and is known as an innovator and thought leader on the subject of talent acquisition.

Greg, when you consider the countless applicants your recruiting team meets each year, what are some of the correctable mistakes you see these job seekers making? And what instead is the better approach?

"I see and hear of a few consistent, but easily remedied, mistakes from job seekers. Here are the main ones with some thoughts on correcting the approach:

- Treating or dismissing the recruiter interview as a formality. Instead: Treat all contacts from the company with the highest degree of equality and respect. People within the organization compare notes to get a complete picture of each candidate. Trust me when I say every interaction with a hiring organization matters.

- Failing to practice responses to common interview questions. Instead: Researching and practicing for your interview is essentially your job right now. Consider it your first test of employment and a way to essentially demonstrate your resourcefulness.
- Not articulating a correlation between their background and the position for which they are interviewing. Instead: Prepare in advance the ways you can parallel your previous experience with the responsibilities outlined for the job. Stick with 2-3 key points and bring notes with you instead of trying to remember the details.
- Trying to connect directly with the hiring manager after establishing contact with the recruiter. Instead: Circumventing anyone in the interview process, trying to go above their head is not a good practice. Think how you would feel in that situation. Would you be an advocate for that candidate? Not likely.
- Aggressively pursuing feedback and next steps from the recruiter after the initial screening has been done. Instead: respect the company's process and allow it to play out. Your urgency to find a job is not in play here. Continue your search throughout this process and even look for temporary or contract work to help ease the financial pressures if you think the job is worth waiting for."

Considering your years of experience in talent management and recruiting, can you speak to the things that "great" candidates do to favorably get your attention?

"Candidates are so varied in how they try and stand out, but sometimes just getting the basics down is important. Here is what candidates can do to positively get our attention during the interview process:

- Establish a professional social media presence/profile.
- Be available as readily as possible.
- Research the company and the interviewers.
- Ensure contact information is current and accurate.
- Ask relevant questions to demonstrate eagerness and interest."

The next interview is with Keith Hicks, the Chief People Officer at MedAssets, a national health care technology and services firm. I have known Keith for a few years and specifically sought him out for his views as an HR leader and as someone who has long invested in helping candidates in job transition.

Keith, what are a few of the biggest trends you have observed the last few years in this job market?

"Although unemployment remains relatively high in most areas of the U.S., the job market is still very tight for top talent. Most employers are looking for people who are already employed and frown upon those who have been unemployed for an extended period of time. It is a bit of a catch-22 for the chronically unemployed. They can't find work because many employers shy away from them due to their long period of unemployment.

"The technology and engineering market has remained hot throughout the last several years. People with technology and engineering backgrounds have not experienced the same levels of unemployment seen in other disciplines. This is also true for people with accounting and finance skills.

"Social media, specifically LinkedIn, has become a very prevalent tool and resource in talent acquisition – both for companies in sourcing candidates and for candidates in networking and finding jobs. Job candidates who are the most successful are taking advantage of these resources to the fullest extent."

What are some things that impress you when a candidate applies for a job or conducts an interview? Any good examples come to mind?

"Knowledge of the company. Learn as much as you can about the company's history, financials (past and present), customers, products and services, culture and values, and the people who work there. I remember a candidate who really impressed me because she not only read through our website and annual report, but she actually visited a customer site and asked questions about our products. That made her stand out.

"There is really no excuse for lacking in knowledge and preparation. I experienced the exact opposite impression of a very enthusiastic candidate who said he had been targeting our company for years. I asked him to tell me what he knew about us and he said, 'Well, not much. I was hoping to learn more during this interview.' Needless to say, this candidate didn't make it to the next interview.

"Interviewing us is critical. The interview process is just as much about the company assessing the candidate as it is about the candidate assessing the company. Many candidates are so eager for the job they fail to properly assess the company. I want to see a candidate being very thoughtful about assessing the company. That means asking questions about the culture, leadership, work environment, and growth opportunities.

"Don't forget to ask about the challenges a company is facing. No company is perfect and it's a fair question to ask. I was very impressed recently when interviewing a candidate who came prepared with many thoughtful questions and told me straight up that she wanted to learn as much as she could about the company to make sure it was a right fit for her and her career.

"Know their own story. Candidates need to be able to articulate the value they bring to an organization, as well as succinctly and confidently share their 'story.' I am often surprised how many candidates cannot tell their own story. They can talk about their skills, knowledge and past job experiences, but the trick is to package all of that up into a compelling value proposition for the hiring manager."

Is there a right or wrong way to work with company hiring managers and internal recruiters?

"There are both, but a specific wrong way comes to mind. Don't be 'open to any opportunity.' Instead, come to the table with a clear idea of your skills and the type of role you are interested in. That will allow you to speak very clearly with hiring managers and internal recruiters about a specific job. Many candidates apply to numerous jobs on a company's website. This is a turnoff because it's clear they are just fishing."

The last interview is with Andy McGowan who conducted his own job search last year before landing in a senior communications role with an international Fortune 200 company. His insights provide a valuable candidate's perspective in working with hiring managers, internal recruiters and search firms.

Andy, not long ago, you went through an extensive job search before finding your current role. Did you work with executive search firms to find the position? What was your experience?

"For my present role, I didn't utilize a search firm. I had been searching online, as well as networking, and was told about the opportunity. I applied online and received a call back within two weeks of my application. I know it was a highly unusual circumstance since my previous experiences with applying for positions online is that they go into a black hole and never see the light of day.

"My experience with corporate recruiters has not been overly positive. The 'don't call us, we'll call you' approach is prevalent. A number of years ago, I went through a search with a large insurance company. It took months to get through the process and I was one of two finalists. The recruiters were not very forthcoming about where we were in the process nor would they provide information on the status of the search. They wouldn't respond to phone calls or emails until they needed me. It was a lot of hurry up and wait.

"So, I had the opportunity when I was running a multi-million dollar business a number of years ago to change that process, at least while I was in charge. I personally responded to every application for employment. I felt that if a person took the time to put together a letter and cover letter, that at least they should receive a response. We were a small company and didn't have an HR department. But, I felt it was important.

"Today, I find that most companies have lost that personal touch. It's apply online, fill in the blanks with all kinds of information – which can take an hour or more to complete –

just to receive an auto-generated response email. And, in most cases you never hear from the company again."

If you were advising someone on how to best work through a search firm, what would you suggest?

"Working through a search firm is different than working with a corporate recruiter. Search firms go through your resume with a fine-toothed comb. Each bullet point that you list on your resume in terms of successes needs a back-up story. The search firm wants to know why you listed that particular point and how it's relevant to their search. As I learned, they take your resume and re-work it to fit the job profile on the position.

"If you're working with a top-flight search company, expect them to check and re-check every line on your resume. And, make sure you have a supporting story for all of your bullet points. The search firm will ask you about each one. And, they will try to put together a picture of your career. They will ask questions like: 'Why did you leave company A to go to company B? What were your areas of responsibility? How were you successful in that role?' Their reputation is on the line just as much as yours, and they want to make sure that they present the best candidates to their client companies.

"The more senior the position, the more you have to be prepared for in-depth questioning. Also, be prepared for multiple interviews before you move on in the process. I was the finalist for a senior-level position working through a very well-known search firm. I had five interviews with the search firm recruiter before being presented to the client. Then, I had two interviews with the client (with the search firm participating), and was told I was the finalist. With the end in sight, I learned that the client hired another candidate – without telling the search firm. That didn't go over well with me, or the search firm. But I learned a lot from the process. It made me hone my career story so that I could give strong answers when I got to the client interview phase."

As you began interviewing with companies, what was your experience like with internal recruiting professionals and hiring managers?

"The best experience I've had with the recruiting process was for a senior-level position that a former colleague recommended me for. Having someone refer you makes the process go much more smoothly. Once my resume was with the company, I was asked to interview. I spent a day with the company interviewing with members of the senior leadership team. It all went well and I was mentally drained after the day, but it paid off as I had an offer 48 hours later.

"If you're recommended to the hiring manager and they are interested in you, my experience is that they will do everything to get you through the process. Of course it's up to you to interview well and demonstrate your worth and value. The hiring manager wants to hire a strong candidate as it makes them look good, too. Personal recommendations along with experience carries a great deal of weight when going through a list of potential candidates.

"The worst experience I've had was when I was going through the process to work for a large Fortune 200 company. The internal recruiters were disorganized and lacked knowledge, even about their own company. As I went through the process, there was an occasion in which they called and asked where I was one afternoon. Supposedly, I was to be interviewing with the leaders of the department for which I applied.

"Unfortunately, the recruiter forgot to tell me about the interview, nor send any information to confirm the meeting. The meeting was rescheduled, but I was both embarrassed and frustrated as they didn't even handle the basic tasks well. As I continued through the hiring process with this company, they continued to do things that I couldn't believe – like not being able to explain the basic benefits package for a potential employee. With another candidate, they actually sent out an offer letter with the wrong person's name on it."

Questions for Reflection:

1. Professional communication and follow-up with all participants in my job search and company interviews is stressed throughout this chapter. How do I rate myself on follow-up and communication? What can I easily improve?

2. Keith Hicks stresses the importance of knowing your "own story. Do I know mine, and can I share it in a succinct and compelling way?

3. Reflecting on my own experiences with internal/external recruiters, search firms and hiring managers, I realize I may need to make changes to my approach. What are those changes and how will I make them?

4. Greg Jackson shared candid observations about what candidates do well and where they make mistakes. How do I stack up against these generalities?

Action Item:

Make a list of every recruiter and hiring manager you encounter and write down all of their contact information and the specific experiences with each one. This could be invaluable if you find yourself in transition in the future.

16 CLOSING THE LOOP

My hope is that by the time you have finished this book or soon after, you are well on the way to landing your next job. When you win the new position, is your job search journey over? Not quite! "Closing the loop" is a critical component of the job search which many candidates ignore. It is completely understandable to want to close this stressful chapter in your life and move on, but a few simple steps can help you project professionalism, courtesy and gratitude to the people who helped you along the way.

You might just be in job transition again someday and need to call upon the same people to help you again.

Here are important best practices to follow as you conclude your job search:

- Send a handwritten thank you note to each person you met with at your new company during the interview process leading to your new job. Email thank you messages are utterly forgettable. Handwritten notes are memorable.
- Call or send a thank you note to each contact who helped you along the way in your job search. Make this time investment. If you are pressed for time and the numbers are

overwhelming, an email is (barely) sufficient, but it is better than doing nothing.

- Consider sending a small gift of appreciation to the people who most went out of their way to help you. Let them know how grateful you are for their help and encouragement. This is especially intended for those who offered job references, and referral sources, mentors and job accountability partners.

- Always remember to help others still in a job search, even though you have Landed a new role. This is a decent act of human kindness which we should all hope others would show toward us.

- Update your LinkedIn profile after you start a new job and inform your extended network of your new email address and other contact information. Email for this type of message is acceptable.

- Remember to show sincere gratitude. You likely didn't get here by yourself.

Seeking additional observations on this idea of closing the loop, I reached out to well-respected human resources executive, Don Sather. Don has invested in helping job seekers for many years and is an integral part of his company's hiring process which made him an excellent resource for this book.

Don, as you consider all the candidates you have interviewed over the years, what were some of the practices that left a positive impression on you?

"Feedback with all constituents in the selection and interview process is critical. Whether during the interviews or after landing the job, those candidates who sent personalized notes thanking me for my time stand out and have always impressed me. I particularly like it when they link something back from our conversation to demonstrate that they were listening to me."

Specifically in the area of communication and follow up, what do you consider as candidate "best practices?"

"One of the best practices I have encountered may seem like common sense in regards to the process, however, it is rarely ever practiced. I want to hear feedback and follow up from the candidate who did <u>not</u> get the job! A simple note from the candidate to the hiring manager thanking them for their time and how much you appreciated meeting them. You can add how someday you would love to work with them and to keep you in mind for future opportunities."

From your experience and observations, is there a right way to close out the process after someone lands a new job? What would you recommend?

"My counsel is that once you have been offered the job and accepted, send your new boss a small thank you gift, such as a leadership book with a personal note on how excited you are about coming to work with him/her and your commitment to the job, etc. Additionally, you should also close out your network that you leveraged during your search process. You could simply send a note to the individuals in your network notifying them on your new contact information and thank them for their assistance in your search efforts."

What about the need to continue networking after you land a new job and also paying it forward for other job seekers?

"I strongly encourage job seekers to always maintain their networks after they land a new role. You never know when you will need these contacts again. Make an investment of time each week, perhaps one coffee meeting, to connect someone in your network. Make this investment and it will pay off in positive ways you won't expect.

"I am a firm believer in paying it forward and nothing bothers me more than to see a candidate land a job and forgot his brothers and sisters on the job battlefield. The favor you do to help others is not only the right thing to do, but it may earn you favors in return one day when you need them."

As I recall the follow-up from candidates I have worked with over the years, the truly grateful ones stick out in my memory. The gifts are nice and appreciated, but the job seekers who took the time to write a personal message and express their thanks not only impressed me, but they will likely win my active assistance in the future if the need it. This is a good lesson to remember!

Questions for Reflection:

1. Have I considered that I might be in the job search again and need my network in the future?
2. Does Don Sather's point about reaching out with thank you notes to the companies who did <u>not</u> hire me resonate?
3. Who in my network is still seeking a job? Who can I invest in and help the way others have kindly assisted me?
4. As I reflect on the search, have I shared my gratitude freely and generously? Can I go back and rectify these mistakes if I have not?

Action Item:

As the chapter advises, make a list of the most important people in your job search network and find a way to thank them, outside of an email. Take the opportunity to be a complete professional with a generous heart and make sure people in your network receive your sincere gratitude.

CONCLUSION

REGAINING YOUR LIFE AFTER LOSING A JOB

When faced with an opportunity to fundamentally change your life, will you take it? Many of us want to answer this question with a resounding "yes," but may think that reality is not attainable. That's not necessarily so. Consider the possibility that the current recession may be providing the catalyst for meaningful lessons and positive life changes to people all around you.

As I have shared throughout this book, I meet dozens of business people every month, many of whom are professionals in transition. My interviews often take the form of an informal dialogue where I invite the job candidate to share not only work experiences, but also how they are feeling and coping with being out of work. The feedback has been illuminating. There are striking similarities in the challenges this group faces after they leave their jobs which fall into three distinct categories: *relevancy, validation* and *balance*.

Uncovering the benefits of these three areas now can benefit your work and entire life for the long term. Life challenges have a way of forcing much needed self-discovery, and what you learn can change your life. Economic, social and political factors will continue to influence the job market in positive and negative ways; this means your focus will be shifted elsewhere again someday. Now is the time to pay attention to the opportunities that lie ahead and here are some ways to do that.

Relevancy

The upside: It's never too late to start. It is a daunting world for the job seeker today. As if the shock of losing a job is not enough, many candidates quickly learn that they have lost some degree of relevancy while plugging away at their former jobs. They have neglected to maintain a network inside as well as outside their places of business. The latest online social networking tools are a mystery. Paradigm shifts in how to effectively reach prospective hiring managers are vastly different from the last time they were on the job market and many have not remained on the leading edge of their industry.

So, why is this important? Long tenures at companies are becoming a rarity. It is likely that you will experience multiple job changes over your career and you need to be prepared for that eventuality. Staying well networked in and out of your organization is critical. Just as important is the need to stay on top of new trends not only in your industry, but in the marketplace in general. The vast majority of job candidates I meet spend the first few months of searching in a steep learning curve attempting to become current and trying to frantically build personal and professional networks they should have been nurturing along the way.

The challenge of staying relevant is not necessarily generational. This issue affects everyone from recent college grads to seasoned professionals. Regardless of your position or years of experience, begin thinking beyond the silo of your current job (or next one) and make a commitment to nurture your professional relationships, be well versed on industry and market trends, and above all, stay relevant when you find yourself in career transition.

Ideas for staying relevant:

1. Build and maintain relationships by having coffee or lunch once a week with someone outside your organization. Do the same with colleagues inside your company.

2. Make your personal and career development a priority. Read books and take courses relevant to your industry and for achieving your personal goals. Attend seminars, workshops, networking events, etc.

3. Utilize social networking tools like LinkedIn and Facebook to manage what should be an ever expanding network. Be visible!

Validation

The upside: There are healthier ways to feel good about yourself! Your boss says you're doing a good job. Clients thank you for delivering great service. Friends in the office tell you they respect your strong work ethic. You are respected in the community and appreciated at home as the person who has it all: great job, wonderful family, strong commitment to stewardship and work/life balance. Each and every day carries with it some form of validation which is directly connected to your self-worth. Then you lose your job …

This loss of personal validation is rarely written about, but often comes up in my discussions with candidates who have been out of work a month or more. At this point reality has set in and often self-worth begins to be adversely affected. The hard lessons of a job loss force many to confront this uncomfortable reality, but there is hope.

Consider these alternate means of validation: "I love you, Dad," "Thanks for coming to my game, Mom, it means a lot to have you here," "I am grateful for your candid advice and appreciate your friendship," or "I really appreciate you helping out with the school play—we couldn't have done this without you." You get the picture. The validation coming from family, friends and your local community can be much more meaningful. A job doesn't define who you are, and you don't want people to remember you with: "He sure had a great career!"

Brandon Smith, founder of "The Workplace Therapist" and who provided the Forward and other great insight for this book, suggests overcoming the challenge of loss of validation through the lens of finding one's purpose. He offered this insight: "Perhaps the greatest antidote to the struggle job seekers face today with validation is purpose. Purpose connects us to the needs we are ultimately trying to meet in the world, either through our job or beyond. Purpose is critical in these times because it gives us a way to proactively make sense out of the world and see how the world needs us today more than ever.

"What a different orientation than most job seekers take. When we have a sense of purpose and lead with that during these times, it allows us to approach companies and tell them how we can help them overcome their struggles today. It can also provide us a channel through which to get validation."

In other words, pursue your passion in your next job and not just a means of making a living.

Ideas for regaining healthy validation:

1. Don't let your work define who you are. If you could write the story of your life, think about how you would make it full of family and friends whose lives you positively impacted.

2. Brandon Smith offered this idea: "Consider your purpose. What need are you trying to meet today in the world? How might companies need you today more than ever? Consider using this to reframe your orientation and your approach to the job search."

3. Pay it forward. Make the effort to help others during your search. Offer candid advice, help with networking, be a good listener.

Balance

The upside: You can rediscover what you should be working for. The most profound difference for many of the job seekers is the re-discovery of the joys of family. They are able to spend quality time with children and get reacquainted. The former drudgery of a heavy travel schedule is transformed into taking the kids to school and relishing every school activity and event. Reconnecting to spouses and reinvigorated marriages are often a result of this job hiatus as couples who only saw each other on weekends are actually required to communicate on a daily basis. Many speak of a newfound sense of community and others talk of a deeper relationship with God. Often, people are finding the personal time they always needed (and never had) to get in shape through exercise and better eating habits. Their lives are coming into balance for maybe the first time in years.

Peter Bregman, CEO of a global leadership and change management consulting firm, wrote an article for *Harvard Business Review* titled, "Need to Find a Job? Stop Looking So Hard." He suggests: "If you're passionate about what you're doing, and you're doing it with other people who are passionate about what they're doing, then chances are the work you eventually find will be more in line with the stuff you love to do. And then your life changes."

To be sure, there are significant stresses during a job search, especially financial pressures to find a new job quickly. But, this respite from the storm is allowing a pendulum swing in a positive direction that many candidates are utilizing as a catalyst to pursue a career and life change. As they look for new jobs, they are intentionally focusing on roles that allow for greater work/life balance and less travel. Climbing the corporate ladder is increasingly taking a backseat to the pursuit of the more fulfilling roles as well-rounded husbands and wives/fathers and mothers.

As Brandon shared, pursuit of your purpose is important. In that context, ask yourself if your work exists to serve your family or if your family exists to serve your work. I have often faced that question in my career and am not always proud of the answer.

My interactions with people in career transition tell me that the majority wrestle with this problem as well.

Ideas for achieving balance:

1. We spend most of our lives at work, but it shouldn't consume most of our lives. Be more intentional in your next job. Make different priorities that will help you achieve balance. For example: a) be home for dinner every night, b) have a new "show up agenda" and attend the kid's activities, c) make time for me—exercise, reading, friends, and d) make date nights and better communication with my spouse a priority.

2. Ask your family and friends to hold you accountable in your pursuit of balance. Get feedback on a frequent basis on how you are doing with balance.

3. Ask yourself from time to time if your work is serving your family and a higher purpose or is it the other way around. It is easy to get lost in the day to day, so course corrections will be needed.

To conclude, I realize I haven't addressed every challenge job seekers face today, nor was that the intent. I simply wanted to share what I have learned from others who may be in similar situations and address the issues they are struggling with both personally and professionally. I encourage us to at least consider the positives that can come from all this and look at new ways to overcome these difficult times.

Our jobs place enormous demands on our time and will consume us if we are not careful. But good things can come of it. Dean Harbry is executive advisor and coach for Internal Innovations, a professional coaching and leadership development firm, and offers: "I have observed a common thread with my displaced clients. They are asking the question, 'What is my purpose, and how can I find a way to live that purpose in my next job?' Times of transition can be more helpful than you realize as you spend time with family, dig deep on what truly motivates you, and validate that notion through the feedback of those around you. Your spouse, children and close friends have a superior vantage point to help you make the next step into more meaningful work."

As you pursue the next job in your career, think about these lessons and be more intentional about staying relevant, seeking healthier validation and leading a more balanced life. Self-discovery can be a little scary, but I hope what I have shared in this book will inspire you and prepare you for the next phase of your life journey. We all need to make a living, but we need to live while we are working. We would all love another chance to "get it right." Maybe this is yours.

APPENDIX ONE

Advice for New College Graduates: An Interview with Gen Y Expert Dr. Tim Elmore, Founder of Growing Leaders

Dr. Tim Elmore and his organization, Growing Leaders (growingleaders.com), have a long and successful track record of developing leadership and character in young people all over the world. Because of his vast experience and insight into the thinking of Generation Y, I interviewed Dr. Elmore for thoughts on how to best prepare this generation for the workforce:

What is your candid advice for recent college graduates in finding jobs in this difficult economy?

Two things. First, be sure your expectations are realistic. Today's graduate enters the toughest market since the Great Depression. Don't lose sight of your dreams for a career, but know you're likely to enter at the bottom of the ladder. All you need to be concerned about is making sure it's the right ladder.

Second, be more conscious of what you can give, than what you will get. Typically, graduates are conditioned to be preoccupied with negotiating salary, benefits and vacation time. All of that's important, but you will be refreshing to employers if they see you are consumed with adding value to the team, not extracting it from the team. Think contributor, not consumer.

Is there a Best and Worst Practices list for approaching the job market which comes to mind when you consider this group?

Yes, as you interview and seek placement in the job market, perform the following balancing acts:

1. Balance confidence with teachability.

Research from a variety of employment sources reveal that 76 percent of young employees believe "my boss can learn a lot from me." That may be true, but any hint of arrogance in the interview may repel a Baby Boomer host. In the interview, know your value and strengths, but communicate a teachable spirit—that you want to learn a lot from your potential employer.

2. Balance warmth with formality.

Often, recent college grads become too informal, joking about personal elements in their lives or about the interviewer themselves. This is risky. Many HR executives believe this is the number one problem with young employees. Some even text or take a phone call during the interview. Instead, be warm and friendly—but remember, these people don't know you yet. Don't lose the chance to go deeper.

3. Balance creativity with cooperation.

Today, 83 percent of new graduates are looking for a place where "my creativity is valued." A full two out of three want to "invent their own position at work." While that is understandable, your new boss may value your helping the company with their current ideas first. Let them know you've got ideas, but you're hungry to help with theirs as well.

4. Balance ambition with humility.

Employers love ambition. Just be sure yours doesn't make you look cocky. Many call this balance, "humbitious." Humble yet ambitious. It's a rare skill set. Two of three 20-somethings believe they should be mentoring older co-workers on how to get things done. Even if this is true, don't say it in the interview. Be humble, get hired, and show them who you are. Folks want to see a sermon not hear one.

5. Balance listening with initiative.

Spend plenty of time on the organization's website and learn all you can. Find out who the key leaders are, and greet them by name when you see them. In the job interview, answer questions clearly and candidly, but then, inquire if it is okay to ask the interviewer a few questions, as well. This usually is impressive. Pose questions that show you've gotten acquainted with their mission. Ask about the future. Embody the values of the organization if possible, demonstrating you'll fit right in.

6. Balance passion with work ethic.

Let me explain this correlation. Half of today's college graduates would rather have "no job" than a job they dislike. Yet, nine of 10 say they'll work very hard if they know where their task is going. Passion marks the Millennial generation. Some employers wonder however: "Will you display work ethic on a project that isn't glitzy? Can you show some passion for the smaller, mundane task you'll do as you stand on the bottom rung of the career ladder?"

Is there a Gen Y success story you can recall of a new job seeker who Landed a great job after graduation? What was different about this person and why do they stand out?

Yes. We have several of them working with us at Growing Leaders. Alysse entered confident yet so mature, affirming positive things she saw in our office, asking good questions and suggesting ideas we could implement even before we hired her. Jim simply blew us away with his "extra-mile" service, arriving early and staying late, just to make sure he didn't slow any other team member down during his learning curve. Chloe was an aggressive "learner" hungry to pick up any wisdom, taking notes at every meeting. Each had a teachable spirit, a hungry mind and a bias for action sold us on them.

What do Baby Boomer and Generation X leaders who are hiring Gen Y for their companies need to know about this group?

There is much for us to learn. We must learn to look past the differences and see the strengths they bring. For instance, they may appear picky, but they just want to do work that makes a difference. They may come across too "social" for your tastes, but they want to work with a community of people that feels like a family.

They may joke around too much, but they don't separate work from play, which means they may do their best work at midnight not noon. (Remember Facebook is their Rolodex). They may come across a bit cocky, but they can probably teach us a few things about technology and social media. What we must do is be open to mutual mentoring—where both the established leader invests in the young employee, and allows that young team member to mentor them as well.

APPENDIX TWO

Job Search 101 for New College Graduates: An Interview with Dr. Jason Aldrich, Executive Director, Career Management Center at Georgia State University's Robinson College of Business

Jason Aldrich has worked in higher education for nearly 20 years and currently serves as Executive Director of the Career Management Center at Georgia State University's J. Mack Robinson College of Business. Before joining GSU, Jason served in similar roles at Vanderbilt University and The University of Georgia.

Because of his experience working with college students and employers, I interviewed Dr. Aldrich for insights on how college students can best prepare for the job search.

How has the downturn changed the job market for college students?

The level of competition has increased significantly. Although the job market for college students has improved significantly since 2008-09, we have not returned to pre-downturn hiring levels for college graduates. As a result, there are two significant trends college students need to be aware of.

The first trend is a backlog of talented recent graduates who are competing for entry level jobs. In fact, many students who completed their undergraduate studies between 2008 to 2010 returned to school and completed graduate degrees. As a result, employers find themselves in a buyer's market where they can be very selective.

The second trend is an increased emphasis by employers to convert interns to full-time hires. Prior to the downturn, internship programs were seen by most employers as a supplement to their full-time college hiring efforts. During the downturn as most employers reduced full-time college hiring significantly, internship programs increasingly became viewed as a cost-effective way to keep the college talent pipeline open. Firms increased their efforts to convert interns to full-time hires as the job market slowly improved.

Today, most firms recruit interns with the goal of converting 60-70 percent to full-time hires. This trend provides current college students with an opportunity to leverage internships that recent graduates don't have access to.

What are employers looking for when they hire recent graduates?

The reality in most organizations today is that new hires have to be able to learn on the fly and connect the dots themselves. As a result, they are seeking students who successfully built the academic knowledge, interpersonal skills and gained the practical experience necessary to hit the ground running in their first professional role. Research indicates team work, integrity, energy, effective use of technology and strong interpersonal skills are key attributes employers seek.

How should recent college students prepare themselves to find their first job?

The key is to make meaningful connections between your academic coursework, co-curricular activities and real world work experiences. By doing so, you are building the competencies employers are seeking. In addition to strong grades and co-curricular activities, today the differentiator for college students is having at least one high-quality internship prior to their senior year.

In fact, going through the process of developing a resume, researching organizations, applying and interviewing for internships mirrors the full-time job search process. In addition, most schools have a wealth of resources available to help college students with the process.

However, college students typically underestimate how long the process of looking for an internship or full-time job will take. The best analogy I have for students to understand how to approach the process is to think of it this way: "You're taking a

3.0 credit class called I need a job, it's the toughest course you've ever taken, and you have to earn an A to pass." The search process requires a consistent amount of effort, it comes with highs and lows, and you need to stay open to feedback. In addition, it often takes two semesters to complete. The best way to accelerate the process is to start as a junior with an internship search.

What specific areas of the job search should students focus on?

Great question! There are five components I encourage students to think about.

1. Identify Your Resources – The first step is to identify the people who can help you develop your job search. Most colleges and universities have career services offices that can provide you with resume writing assistance, access to job postings, workshops, career fairs and campus interviews. In addition, students should also consider student clubs, alumni events and networking with their professors as important resources to explore. Last, but not least, this is a great time to ask family and friends for input as well.

2. Know Thyself – After you identify your resources, the next step is learning how to communicate how your interests, abilities and unique experiences can add value to an organization. Sounds simple, but this takes some work because you have to be able to relay this message to a variety of audiences in many forms (i.e., resume, LinkedIn, networking meetings and interviews). Too often this is where college students don't spend enough time. Gaining clarity in this area will accelerate the job search.

3. Develop a Strategy –The best approach is to identify and apply for a variety of opportunities using multiple methods. For example, career fairs are fairly standard events at most colleges. Research the firms in advance, identify your top 10, but visit other firms as well. Also, most schools host campus interviews and have their own job posting systems. Openings posted at your school often come from alumni or firms who have historically hired graduates from your

college. Make the most of these opportunities, but also spend time networking for jobs through the other resources you've identified. This is an area where college students often struggle. Be careful not to focus on a very small number of firms, a limited geographic area, or apply to too many openings online without engaging in networking.

4. Research the Employer – Year after year, the number one complaint we hear from employers who interview students is how poorly they research the organization. Firms find this frustrating because of the wealth of information they make available to candidates and the additional information that is available online. One of the easiest ways to differentiate yourself during the job search is to research the organization – we hear this time and again, but there is still a disconnect here. By knowing their products, competitors, growth plans and how the role you're interviewing for fits into the organization's overall plans you will be a step ahead. Vault, Bloomberg and Forbes are just a few places to start.

5. Prepare for the Interview – An interview is an opportunity to show the organization how you can help them achieve their goals. The best way to stand out from the competition is to make connections between your abilities and the employer's needs. The next step is to anticipate the types of questions they are most likely to ask and be prepared to provide examples from your background that demonstrate you have the experience necessary for the role. I strongly recommend engaging in a videotaped practice interview in order to polish your interview skills. InterviewStream.com is a great tool for this.

What advice would you give college students as they enter the workplace?

Two pieces of advice stick out in my mind:

1. *It's not a smart contest.* One of the interesting shifts that occurs as college students enter the workplace is recognition that success is often more about consistent effort, working in teams, and learning on the fly than it is about where you

went to school or who earned the best grades. In addition, much of the day-to-day work that has to get done, particularly at the entry level is not very glamorous. Understanding that getting "grunt work" done and doing so with enthusiasm is often the only way you get a chance to do more interesting work. This is an important factor in the early stages of your professional development.

2. *Go where the pain is.* Find out where the organization is experiencing big problems and figure out how to fix them. This is one way to advance quickly, which may seem counter-intuitive, but I've seen it work many times.

APPENDIX THREE

Options for Professional Women in Today's Workforce: An Interview with Nicole Siokis, President of Mom Corps Atlanta

Nicole, I have known you for years and you have always been passionate about flexibility and better options for women in the workforce. Talk about the importance of that.

The idea of flexibility is not just a "mommy issue" although we are the group that tends to be most vocal about wanting and needing flexibility. Time and again, I talk with women who need to work for financial reasons or want to work because they enjoy it, but still need some sort of flexibility to accommodate other obligations.

Unfortunately, many have a hard time finding the "perfect" job that allows them to work and gives them the flexibility they want. I experienced it first hand when working at a Fortunate 500 company where even talking about flexibility was taboo. Achieving work-life synergy and overall workplace flexibility is on the minds of many employees.

In our 2013 Labor Day survey we were pleasantly surprised by the following results:

- Three out of four (75%) of working adults report having "at least a little" flexibility at work—a significant increase compared to 68% in 2012 and 64% in 2011.
- Seventy-three percent of working adults agree that flexibility is one of the most important factors they consider when looking for a new job or deciding what company to work for—a more than 10 percentage point increase from 2012 (61%) and 2011 (62%) reports.
- More than two in three (68%) working adults agree that their company would be willing to accommodate them if they requested a flexible work schedule, due to reasons like family care, personal work preferences, health issues, etc.

- Eighty percent of working adults agree that flexible work options are just as important for people who don't have children as they are for those who do, and interestingly, there is no significant difference in opinion between women (69%) and men (66%).
- When asked if they would be willing to give up a portion of their salary for more flexibility at work, 45 percent of U.S. working adults said they would be willing to relinquish at least some portion of their salary—consistent with the findings of both 2012 (45%) and 2011 (42%).
- Nearly three in four (73%) working adults believe it is possible to "have it all" when it comes to work/life balance, a slight increase from 2012 reports, in which 67 percent of working adults felt that way.

Have you seen the workplace become more open to this idea?

Absolutely. We still have a long way to go, but we are definitely gaining momentum in workplace flexibility because people are openly talking about it more now. Many smaller to mid-size businesses recognize the top talent they can attract at a reduced cost, just by offering flexibility. We're seeing more companies offer a greater variety of flexible options as well.

Even more encouraging is some large corporations, like consulting giant, McKinsey, are openly wooing back their women alumni with flexible work arrangements because they are painfully aware of the impact of turnover by a highly educated, hardworking talent pool.

Why is it good for companies to embrace the idea of a flexible and part time workforce?

First, it is important to understand that flexibility means different things to different people and companies. It can manifest as a flex work schedule (i.e., part time, flex hours), it can involve a shorter daily commute or less overall travel. It doesn't require an employer to allow all employees to work from home 100 percent of the time. Studies by the Family and Work Institute have shown that companies who embrace a flexible work environment have higher employee engagement and significantly lower turnover and absenteeism than their counterparts who do not embrace a flexible workplace. This directly impacts a company's profitability.

A recent study showed the average cost of absenteeism for a company of 150 employees is $208,000 per year. So, if implementing a remote policy decreased absenteeism by as much as 17.5 percent, it could save a company $36,400 per year. AFLAC's call center saw retention rates go from 87 to 94 percent over two years after introducing alternate schedules.

In our Mom Corps annual workplace survey we found: *Fifty-two percent of working adults would be interested in starting their own business in order to achieve a better work-life balance, led by men age 35-44 (75%).* That potential for turnover should be a wakeup call for many businesses. As companies look at tighter margins and reduced profitability, it makes sense that the topic of flexibility is key to long-term financial success.

What advice do you have for a job seeker looking for more flexibility in their career? What about for women returning to the workforce after their children grow older?

I have five specific pieces of advice on this based on a great deal of experience

1. Research flex-friendly companies online. Here are a few of our favorite online resources:

   - WorkingMother.com has several "Best Companies" lists including: 100 Best Companies for Working Moms,
   - NAFE/Flex-Time Lawyers Best Law Firms for Women
   - Best Companies for Hourly Workers
   - Glassdoor.com lists the "Top 25 Companies for Work-Life Balance."
   - CNNMoney.com has a yearly list of "100 Best Companies to Work For" that you can sort by perks such as Best Companies for Work-Life Balance and Best Companies for Telecommuting.

2. Check out smaller companies. We often find that smaller companies are more willing to accommodate flexibility

needs as they realize the business advantages of a flexible workforce. With a smaller company, there's often less red-tape and cultural barriers to overcome in your pursuit of flexible work.

3. Try researching companies you're interested in to see what their policies are regarding workplace flexibility. Chances are, they might already allow some forms of flexible work, but don't necessarily advertise it as such. Visit the website and see what kinds of positions they are offering and investigate their work environment and policies. Typically, companies that support "ROWE" (results-oriented work environments) champion workplace flexibility.

4. Reach out to your network. Do you know anyone with a flexible job? If so, talk to them about how they found the job, or negotiated for flexibility. These conversations can be extremely insightful.

5. Be willing to do some contract or temp work. This is the key to "getting your foot in the door" and gaining work experience that you may not otherwise have gotten. According to CareerBuilder, 35 percent of the companies that are hiring temporary or contract workers this year have plans to eventually fill or create full-time positions. If a permanent job opens up, it makes sense that the employer would first consider a well-vetted, well-liked temp over an unknown entity.

Are there any recommendations to best pursue flexibility in your career?

The Families and Work Institute defines "workplace flexibility" as enabling employees to exercise some measure of control over when, where and how much they work. By their definition, workplace flexibility must "work" for the employee and the employer alike. Second, know your options for flexibility and figure out what it is that you really want and need:

1. Time: One common misconception is that a flexible job is a part-time job. However, flexible refers to the flexing of the work schedule. We talk about alternative methods of work time as including modified daily hours, a modified

workweek, and working part-time or something other than Monday through Friday, 9 to 5.

2. Place: Where and how work is performed can also lead a job to be classified as flexible. Some variations of place include telecommuting some days. For some candidates, a flexible job in their field would mean they simply wouldn't be required to travel for business all the time. For others, a shorter commute would make a job more flexible – regaining hours of their day due to the proximity of the job to their home.

3. Duration: The jobs we source vary from permanent (with no anticipated end date), temporary (contract, with an end date in mind), project-based (working until the project is considered complete by the employer), or seasonal. One example of a flexible job based on duration is the accountant who wishes to work only during tax season (perhaps working full time or more), and then having the rest of the year off. Or the professional who prefers to work from project to project, contract to contract with no permanent commitment.

Once you know what form of flexibility you are looking for (time, place or duration, or some combination thereof), do your research. Seek out mentors who have that flexibility and learn how they make it work. Look into your own company's options. Consult the HR department to see what is available or if there are ways to approach your manager about obtaining the flexibility you desire. If that approach doesn't work, hiring managers often are open to the discussion of workplace flexibility if your skill set is especially right for the position.

You might be surprised at the options available to you. As you build trust with your manager, you may earn the increase in flexibility over time as well. If your current situation does not offer the flexibility you need then a change may be in order. If that is the case, research the companies and industries that offer the best flexibility options (refer to the list above). The bottom line is that you can never have the flexibility you want or need without asking for it. Be prepared for a potential compromise because the solution has to work for both the employee and the employer.

APPENDIX FOUR

Helpful Resources

Research Websites:

www.salary.com

www.zoominfo.com

www.job-hunt.org

www.rileyguide.com

www.glassdoor.com

Job Search Engine Websites:

www.Indeed.com

www.SimplyHired.com

www.LinkUp.com

Networking Websites:

www.LinkedIn.com

www.beyond.com

Job Board Websites:

www.monster.com

www.careerbuilder.com

www.LinkedIn.com

www.vault.com

www.TheLadders.com

www.hotjobs.yahoo.com

Online Video Training for Interviews:

www.SpotlightPerformance.com

Spotlight Performance is an Atlanta-based technology and performance improvement firm. Their centerpiece product is a web application—a robust coaching tool that lets you use video to train, practice and prepare for professional interactions.

Free Resume Templates/Help Websites:

http://career-advice.monster.com/resumes-cover-letters/resume-samples/sample-resumes-by-industry/article.aspx

http://www.careerperfect.com/content/resume-writing-help-sample-resumes/

ABOUT THE AUTHOR

With a 25+ year career in business operations, corporate recruiting and executive search, Randy Hain has an established track record of leading successful teams and working with a national group of diverse clients in a broad spectrum of industries.

As the founder and president of Serviam Access, (www.serviamaccess.com) he has built a vibrant national network built on authenticity and trust and is well known for connecting professionals and his targeted relationship coaching. As a partner and shareholder of Bell Oaks Executive Search (www.belloaks.com), Randy has worked with clients on a national level in filling leadership roles ranging from individual contributor to C-level executive.

He has developed a stellar reputation in the Atlanta and national business community for integrity, thought leadership, building relationships, successful execution and innovative talent strategy.

Randy is board chair of Growing Leaders, an international non-profit focused on developing leadership and character in young people, advisory board chair for the Catholic Charities Atlanta Leadership Class and an advisory board member for Jamstir.com. He is also an advisory board member for Hire Dynamics. Randy is a co-founder of the Annual Atlanta Catholic Business Conference and the Integrated Catholic Life eMagazine.

He is the author of three other books - The Catholic Briefcase: Tools for Integrating Faith and Work, Along the Way: Lessons for an Authentic Journey of Faith and his latest: Something More: The Professional's Pursuit of a Meaningful Life.

Randy is a prolific writer and contributing blogger to The Huffington Post and National Catholic Register. Randy is a 1989 graduate of the University of Georgia and is married with two sons.

Made in the USA
Lexington, KY
08 December 2013